Original Blessing

Original Blessing

Putting Sin in Its Rightful Place

Danielle Shroyer

Fortress Press
Minneapolis

ORIGINAL BLESSING
Putting Sin in Its Rightful Place

Copyright © 2016 Fortress Press. All rights reserved. Except for brief
quotations in critical articles or reviews, no part of this book may be
reproduced in any manner without prior written permission from the
publisher.

Visit http://www.augsburgfortress.org/copyrights/ or write to
Permissions, Augsburg Fortress, Box 1209, Minneapolis, MN 55440.

Unless otherwise noted, scripture quotations are from the New Revised
Standard Version Bible, copyright (c) 1989 by the Division of Christian
Education of the National Council of the Churches of Christ in the USA.
Used by permission. All rights reserved.

Cover design: Brad Norr

Library of Congress Cataloging-in-Publication Data
Print ISBN: 978-1-4514-9676-5
eBook ISBN: 978-1-5064-2029-5

The paper used in this publication meets the minimum requirements of
American National Standard for Information Sciences — Permanence of
Paper for Printed Library Materials, ANSI Z329.48-1984.
Manufactured in the U.S.A.

This book was produced using Pressbooks.com, and PDF rendering was
done by PrinceXML.

Life's great happiness is to be convinced we are loved.
—*Victor Hugo, Les Misérables*

Contents

Introduction: Elevator Pitch ix

I. AWAKENING TO BLESSING

Blessing is Like Bulletproof Glass 3

Blessing is God's Prerogative 11

Original Sin is Unnecessary and Unhelpful 25

A Tale of Two Boxes and a Golden Thread 47

II. REVISITING THE GARDEN

Let's All Take a Deep Breath about Genesis 59

God's Actions Speak Loudly of Blessing 75

You Can't Rush Happily Ever After 87

III. RETHINKING SIN

East of Eden 113

We're Blankets, Not Sheets of Steel   131

We All Live Downstream   141

Bodies, Babies, and Baptism   153

IV. REDISCOVERING JESUS

Why Do We Need Jesus?   167

Why the Cross is a Blessing   177

V. LIVING INTO BLESSING

Practice, Not Perfect   195

Serpents, Doves, and Eyeglasses   205

Acknowledgments   215

Bibliography   217

Introduction: Elevator Pitch

A pastor and a priest step into an elevator. I was the pastor; the priest was a new friend I'd made at a conference. We'd been jovially debating theology for a few hours in the conference hotel restaurant, my friends and I in our jeans and T-shirts, and him in his sturdy white collar and crisp black shirt, ever the priest even at last call at the hotel bar. As we stepped onto the elevator, I mentioned that I was writing a book about original blessing. Surprised, he asked, "Wait, so you don't believe in original sin?" I laughed. "No, I definitely do not."

His eyebrows raised incredulously as he said, in all seriousness, "Then why do we need Jesus?"

I get it. We've been told over and over again that we need Jesus because of our sin. We don't even question whether this is the best or most genuine description of the gospel anymore. We've heard it so many times we accept it without thinking.

You've heard of an elevator pitch, where in twenty to thirty seconds you compellingly describe and spark interest about someone or something. Eventually, your elevator pitch becomes what you're known for. It becomes your identity, your reputation. If you ask a stranger on the street what Christians believe, you'll hear an answer that doesn't just include sin but considers sin the headline.

Sin plays a starring role in Christianity's elevator pitch.

But it shouldn't.

It makes following Jesus sound like the sin version of tax evasion. It makes faith the sum total of a get-out-of-hell-free card. And worst of all, it frames the gospel as a story of separation.

There's a well-worn description of the great chasm of sin, where we're on one side and God is on the other, and Jesus' cross provides a bridge over which we can walk to God again. That illustration isn't a description of the gospel. It's a description of the story of original sin. And original sin is not the gospel.

The gospel is not a story of us being separated by sin from God. It's the story of a God who is so faithfully *for* us and intent on being *with* us that God became human to help us embody the wholeness and fullness of life we've been made for. It's not a story of separation. It's a story of invitation and participation.

At some point along the way, we Christians took a wrong turn; that turn is the doctrine of original sin. For about 1500 years now, we've kept going, doubling down on the fork we took in the road. And rather than turning back or getting directions or even deciding that we'd traveled far enough, we just kept going. Original sin took us down the wrong path. It took us into a version of the gospel where sin is the headline and separation is the norm. We are long overdue for a turnaround.

That turnaround is *original blessing*. Far more than just being made in God's image, original blessing claims we are steadfastly held in relationship with God. Original blessing reminds us that God calls us *good* and *beloved* before we are anything else. Sin is not at the heart of our nature; blessing is. And that didn't stop being true because Adam and Eve ate fruit in the garden. In fact, it has never stopped being true.

Original sin tells us there is a chasm of separation between humanity and God. And this chasm isn't just some cosmic reality; it exists within our own nature. When you think about it that way, a bridge hardly seems sufficient. We might be able to walk across the bridge and stand next to God, but the sin nature that supposedly separates us from God is coming right along with us. If our human nature separates us from God, we need more than a bridge. We need to be disembodied, which is a weird place to end up in a faith that's based on God becoming human.

When we claim a sin nature, we depart the green pastures and still waters of blessing for the dry desert chasm of separation. We forfeit walking with our shepherd, and walk across his back to get our salvation ticket validated instead. But Jesus doesn't want us to walk across him. He wants us to walk with him.

The gospel is not a solution to our sin problem. It's an invitation to participate in the blessing and life of God. And that is fantastic news. It's headline news. It's a compelling elevator pitch.

Original blessing is one of the most beautiful gifts Christianity has to offer the world. While there's nothing original about sin, original blessing is truly revolutionary. In a world too often bent on retribution, original blessing is the healing balm of God's faithful and unending love.

We may be steeped in years of a bad elevator pitch, but that doesn't mean we can't change it. My Lebanese grandmother knits, and she can intertwine colors and patterns to make a beautiful blanket without even looking down at her hands. She's had a lot of practice, but sometimes she misses. I called her one day and she answered the phone all in a huff. I asked her what was wrong and she said she had spent a few hours knitting a blanket, only to realize she had gotten off her line and the pattern was just crooked the whole way down after that. "What did you do?" I asked. "Honey!" she said in her thick accent. "There's only one thing I could do. I had to unstitch it all the way back to there and start over again."

It can be scary and frustrating and disheartening to realize that we need to rethink much of what we thought we had figured out, but turning around is a central aspect of the Christian faith. It's called repentance. Rather than continuing to walk down the wrong road, rather than settling for a crooked blanket or a bad elevator pitch, rather than feeling resigned to a story of our life with God that's couched in separation, we can choose to turn toward a life grounded in blessing. That turn changes our entire journey. It's amazing what transformation can happen when we see the world through the lens of blessing.

The biggest, most revolutionary, most important gift God

has ever given us is blessing. Without blessing, we would not exist. Without blessing, we wouldn't know grace, or mercy, or forgiveness. Without blessing there is no steadfast love, no covenant, no Jesus, no Spirit, no kingdom of God. The universe may have started with a big bang, but our relationship with God started with blessing.

And it's time we tell that beautiful story.

I. Awakening to Blessing

Blessing is Like Bulletproof Glass

My first job after seminary was as an assistant chaplain in a retirement community. I mostly worked in the memory wing for residents with Alzheimer's disease. Every Thursday and Saturday, I would walk up and down the halls with my little black Book of Common Prayer, offering conversation, prayer, and scripture reading to whoever was interested. I soon learned the favorite psalms and verses of certain residents, and many of them would ask for me to read the same lines over and over again, often closing their eyes as if to let the words wash over them. There was Psalm 23, of course, and Psalm 100, and Psalm 121. But no words of scripture brought the same response as Isaiah 43:1.

As a young and inexperienced pastor, I felt overwhelmed by the enormity of being charged with saying something holy or profound at life's most critical moments. What do I say in the face of loss, grief, confusion, and, oh my God, death? My chaplain and friend, Robin, had highlighted Isaiah 43:1 and earmarked it, too, as if to say, "This. Read this." (And maybe otherwise just keep your mouth shut.) And I did.

At those moments where a resident felt profoundly lost and disoriented, unaware of who he was or where he was, I read it. When a husband lost his wife of sixty years, I read it. To a daughter who just lost her beloved mother, I read it. I read it in the hospital and the infirmary and by bedsides and in Wednesday chapel, and once, on a bench with a man who believed he was waiting for a train to Paris. I read it, because it was the most important thing they needed to know. I believe it is the most important thing any of us need to know.

> But now thus says the Lord,
> God who created you,
> God who formed you:
> Do not fear, for I have redeemed you;
> I have called you by name, you are mine.

God who created you, Ms. Abney. God who formed you, Mr. Croft. God has called you by name. And you belong to God.

You are mine. You belong.

It is the most important thing we need to know. And that's not because there is something fragile or overly sentimental about our human nature. It is because our human nature is designed to belong, and, specifically, to belong to God.

God is our home. We are at home in God.

I was recently at coffee with my friend Christian talking about God. He is bright and passionate and thoughtful, and if his relationship with God was a Facebook status, it would read, "It's complicated." He's not sure he believes in God at all, while I am quite sure I can't *not* believe in God. We pondered this existential predicament over our coffee mugs.

He wanted to know how I could be so sure. I told him it isn't really about being sure; I have my doubts about plenty of things, just like anyone else. It's actually much more invasive than that. Where is there not God? Where even would that be? I couldn't imagine. From my vantage point, all of life is connected to God. Every last bit of it, down to every last atom. That connection is complex and rich and unfathomable, but I have never once doubted there *is* one.

When I read the story of creation in Genesis, I see a story that tells us the foundation of everything else we need to know. We not only learn that we are created by God, and we are good, which is beautiful news. But also, and more fundamentally, we are in a relationship with God that is both benevolent and unwavering, at least from the direction of God to us. (The other direction gets more complicated, which we'll get to later.) All of creation is in relationship with God the Creator, and for reasons unfathomable to me as much as I imagine they are to you, God has decided to stick with it. The animal skins God provides to clothe Adam and Eve is God sticking with it. The rainbow is God sticking with it. The covenant is God sticking with it. The exodus is God sticking with it. The wilderness is God sticking with it. The promised land is God sticking with it. The prophets are God sticking with it. The judges are God sticking with it. Jesus is God sticking with it. Those disciples are God sticking with it. Pentecost is God sticking with it. Revelation is God sticking with it. This story begins with God-with-us and ends with God-with-us, and everything that happens in between declares God-with-us, including but not limited to God's own son.

In every conversation I have had with someone about spiritual things, I have never once wondered whether God is with that person. Does God approve of everything that person does? No. I tend to think God should have given humans some kind of disclaimer label: "The views expressed herein do not necessarily express the views of the Creator." But the idea that someone is outside of God? Where would that outside be, exactly? If we go to the depths, God is there; if we rise to the heavens, God is there. Where can we go from God's presence?

God is sticking with it. God is sticking with us.

Not in a neutral way, either. God is not just along for the ride, or ambivalent. God is with us, and that presence is at the heart of every good and perfect thing, every grace, every single breath of life. That's original blessing. It is nothing less than the anchoring conviction that God is with us. Our relationship with God may be, like it is for my friend, complicated. And let's be honest, God's relationship with us is complicated, too. But to my mind, it is never a relationship that is in question.

Before anything else is true about us—before we can talk about what we are good at or what we are bad at, what we loathe and what we favor, before we can talk about gifts or struggles, virtues or vices, before we can even begin to talk about what it might mean for us to be saved—what is true is that we are in a relationship with God, and God started it. And God is sticking with it.

I believe that is true more fervently than I believe anything else.

Here is something else that is true: God sticks with it, and sometimes we do, too. When that happens, when that glorious harmony sings out, we use words like righteousness and faithfulness and epiphany and redemption and the reign/realm/kingdom of God to describe it. Most Christians would agree this is the goal of life, to live in right relationship with God.

Other times, we don't. Sometimes we simply refuse. Sometimes we choose not to stick with it, because we've decided to stick with something else instead. Some people have never stopped to think about what it is they're sticking with at all, so their lives look more like meandering loops than intentional choices. Sometimes we want to stick with it, and even try, but for whatever reason, we can't. Our wills fail us, and we find ourselves doing the very thing we don't want to do. Paul explained this feeling with dramatic fervor when he wrote, *Who will rescue me from this body of death?!* (Romans 7:24).

Every religion in the world lives at the intersection of the presence of the divine and the reality of humanity. What a beautiful, wondrous mess. If you ask me, every interesting thing comes from this intersection. It is THE intersection, the crossroads from which everything else proceeds.

How we talk about that intersection is of vital importance. It determines how we see God, how we see ourselves, how we treat others, what we value, how we react to success and failure, what we believe we're capable of, and whether we are at peace or not. It determines whether we grow and mature, or whether we give up and give in. It determines what kind of person we become, and what kind of communities we become, and therefore what kind of society we become, and what kind of world we become.

We are a people who live at the intersection of the presence of God and the realities of humanity. What are we going to do about it?

For two thousand years now, Christians have been talking about that. We have debated it, discussed it, written creeds about it, parsed it out in painstaking detail, written millions of pages of theology about it, and started communities of faith to encounter it weekly. It gives us plenty to ponder. What words do we use to describe our relationship with God?

Over the years, sometimes dramatically and other times in subtle ways, we have shifted from telling a story marked by connection to declaring a story marred by distance. And especially in the West, our description of and emphasis on the distance has grown more and more severe.

I believe that is nothing short of a tragedy.

More than any other idea, the doctrine of original sin has slowly eroded our understanding of our relationship with God. Rather than seeing our lives as naturally and deeply connected with God, original sin has convinced us that human nature stands not only at a distance from God but also in some inborn, natural way as contrary to God.

If our relationship with God is the most important one we have, I don't think it wise to discredit it or describe it in negative terms.

I was talking with my friend Carter about this, and he said, "So you mean you want us to see the glass as half full instead of half empty?" My answer is yes . . . and no. If you happen to see the glass as half empty, meaning you focus primarily on the relationship you may or may not have with God, I'll consider it a huge step forward if you begin to see it as half full instead, where at the very least you acknowledge that God is in relationship with you. I think it would be enormously helpful and healthier for you.

But actually, I want you to see the glass differently altogether. I want you to turn your attention not to the contents but to the glass. Our relationship with God is not *in* the glass. It IS the glass. So it's not a matter of half full or half empty. God's relationship to us is not in question. And the glass is there regardless of our response to God. The contents, and how we see them, is our response to God. They can be half full, half empty, brimming over, bone dry, three-quarters full. The contents can be cloudy, crystal clear, delicious, poisonous, questionable, or refreshing. Regardless, the glass is there. It hasn't shattered, or cracked, or begun to leak. It's bulletproof. It still holds you, like it holds everything else. Even in scripture when God is frustrated and angry with people, it's a sign that God is committed. Nowhere in scripture does it say, "Such and such happened, and God was indifferent about it." God is never indifferent about it. Consider it yet another sign that God's sticking with it.

God's relationship with you is fully intact. Your relationship with God may differ from day to day, but it is never located anywhere far away or at a distance. You are not way down here and God is not way up there. You are in God, and God surrounds you. Do not doubt that God holds you, and do not doubt for one minute that God loves you.

I've spent a good deal of time as a pastor talking with people who are on the outs with God. I've been there, too. No relationship of consequence has ever totally avoided conflict, and our relationship with God is no different. Luckily, scripture is filled with stories of people who go through rocky times with God. And what scripture shows is a God who is faithful, even when we're not. So though I don't know what kind of names you might be calling God at the moment, I wholeheartedly believe God calls you by name every moment. Fidelity and steadfast love are God's main character traits. We misunderstand everything if we don't begin there, especially when we're feeling on the outs with God.

We belong to God. That is the center of our identity, the ground of our knowing anything else. If we want to know God, we can only know God through the relationship God has freely initiated with us already. If we want to know ourselves, we start in the same place. Who we are, before anything else, more than anything else, is children of God.

We are people in relationship with a God who is sticking with it. Which is to say, we are all recipients of the gift of original blessing.

Blessing is God's Prerogative

When God spun the world into existence, all of creation was anointed with goodness. God bestowed this anointing, or blessing, before creation had done anything at all. We were simply blessed *as is*. That's hard for us to understand, because we are so used to goodness being connected to our actions. Think of the way we use that word in our daily lives: he is a good soccer player, she is good at her job, that was a good idea, they are good-looking. What we have forgotten is that goodness is both an origin and a goal.

Goodness is an origin in the most literal sense: it's how we begin. We have life only because God has blessed us with it, and when God blesses us with it, it is with grace and steadfast love. God doesn't give life in any other way. Original blessing is simply what happens when God steadfastly decides to be in relationship with us. That relationship bestows goodness upon us, and also within us. We are steadfastly and benevolently tethered to God.

Goodness is also a goal, because it's something we become, too. From our origin of goodness, we can grow into and live into the goodness God intends for us. So original blessing isn't just a state of being, but also a process of becoming. We could say blessing *is*, and blessing *unfolds*. If we think again of the glass metaphor, the glass describes blessing as it is, and the contents describe blessing as it unfolds. Blessing unfolds only because blessing surrounds it. That surrounding gift is original blessing. It is unbreakable, unshakeable, indestructible. From that gift, a world of other blessings can flourish.

If we forget our origin in God, our identity and sense of dignity become reliant on the swirling, ever-changing contents of the glass. Those are stormy and uncertain seas. If we focus on our own view of ourselves, or how other people view us, or how we think the world perceives us, we will be tossed constantly from one sentiment to the next. Some people have a view of God that feels just as stormy, and that's the most problematic of all. If we can't trust the steadfast love God has for us, we will also be tossed around by our questions of whether God finds us worthy or disgraceful, whether we are measuring up or letting God down. But God's relationship to us is not in question. God is sticking with it. So we can find some stability even in the midst of our ever-changing lives by focusing on original blessing above all else.

We can either build our self-worth on the shifting sand of human opinion (including our own), or we can build it on the rock of God's steadfast commitment to us. Our connection to God stabilizes us and allows us the opportunity to flourish. There is no need for us to strive for something that has been right here with us all along. And we falter when we believe we are working against ourselves, instead of acknowledging that we can work with God in our goodness. We can, because we are designed for it and called to it, and God's blessing rests upon us every step of the way.

When I was a junior in high school, I started to get the feeling that I was supposed to go into ministry. Sometimes we describe this as being called; to me it felt more like being summoned, and I wasn't at all sure I wanted to go. I spent much of my senior year pondering (and, to be honest, evading) this potential call, and I remember coming into the kitchen one day to talk about it with my mom. I told her I was struggling with the idea that this feeling of being called into ministry was legitimate, because it didn't make any sense. I didn't really fit in church, and I wasn't your typical church girl. I was loud, and opinionated, and I enjoyed debates far more than I enjoyed quiet agreement, for starters. I continued to list reasons. My mom continued to listen. Then she looked at me and said, "Well honey, if God wanted a girl like that, God would have called one. But God called you. So maybe God doesn't want you to change. Maybe God called you *because* of who you are." When she spoke those words, it was as if a hook snagged my heart and tugged at it. I had felt so much resistance to the idea of changing who I was in order to fit into ministry. I had never once considered that God wanted ministry to find its fit in me. God didn't want me to work against myself. God wanted me to do ministry the only way I could—in my own skin.

Original blessing means we don't have to believe we must work against our human nature to live with God. Our human nature is not an obstacle to our relationship with God. Our humanity is the very reason we're able to have a relationship with God in the first place. Faith guides what we do and how we live, of course, but it does not ask us to diminish or vilify our humanity in the process.

A Circle of Blessing

If you look at the verb "to bless" in Hebrew, *barak*,[1] you see it used in three primary ways: God blessing people, people blessing people, and people blessing God. It's a beautiful description of blessing itself, actually, to see the blessing come full circle. We see how the relationship God begins with us is meant to send us out in love toward others, and also return us back to the heart of God.

Barak is used most frequently when God blesses humanity or creation. At its heart, blessing is an invitation into relationship with God, to abide in God's goodness. When we do so, we experience the fullness of life. Like I said earlier, original blessing is the proclamation that we are in a relationship with God, and God started it.

The second most common use of *barak* is with people blessing other people. When we live in relationship with others, we find our hearts turned toward one another in love. We bless each other. We don't do this outside of the blessing God has given us, but because of it. When we pray, we are

---

1. Some biblical scholars have mistakenly related *BRK* with the verb "to kneel," and even sometimes with the noun "pool," but they are in fact all separate unrelated words. See Christopher Wright Mitchell, *The Meaning of BRK 'To Bless' in the Old Testament* (Atlanta: Scholars, 1987).

pulling the strands that connect us with God and the strands that connect us to the person for whom we are praying. The blessing hums in each direction. We can see blessing at work in the passing of the peace, too. When we extend our hands to one another and say, "The peace of Christ be with you," we are calling that person to a relationship with God that will mean peace also to others. When we say, "The Lord be with you," and respond, "And also with you," we are reminding one another of the blessing of God's presence and relationship with us. When we declare after confession that we are forgiven, we are turning away from our own shame and regret and focusing once again on the free blessing of God's grace. Of course, there are so many other ways we bless each other, too. When we lay a comforting hand on someone who is hurting, or check in on someone who is going through a difficult time, or share in someone's joy, we are connecting with the love that binds us all together.

The third (and least frequent) way the verb *barak* is used is in praising God, or calling upon others to praise God. We invite people into a relationship of gratefulness, a posture we see commonly in the Psalms. It's our way of saying, "Look what God has done! I am going to bless God. Come, join me!" When our hearts overflow with gratefulness, we find ourselves thanking God and praising God. We bless God, thanks to the blessing God has first given us. My children attend an Episcopal school, so they go to chapel every day. The church I pastored was a good deal more casual than the liturgy they hear at school five days a week, but we always ended our gathering by standing and saying a benediction together. When we finished, my son nearly always added (in a loud voice, like it's his unspoken liturgical job), "Let us bless the Lord!" He first said it out of sheer habit, but there's a reason those Episcopalians say it so often. When we are sent out as God's people after we gather, we are called to bless God with our lives. God blesses us, and we send that blessing onto others and reflect it right back to God. That's blessing, coming full circle.

In all cases, the Hebrew scriptures describe blessing as part of the natural order of things. Blessing isn't magical or even supernatural. A blessing doesn't confer some kind of special power. It simply affirms a preexisting, primary relationship with God. Perhaps the most well-known scriptural blessing comes from Numbers 6:24–26, which says, "The Lord bless you and keep you, the Lord make his face to shine upon you and be gracious to you, the Lord lift up his countenance upon you, and give you peace." This is a blessing, not a petition. We don't have to convince God, because God has already decided to be a God of blessing, of grace, and of peace. Instead, this blessing calls us to remember the gifts of blessing God has for us, respond to them, and acknowledge what the gifts will do. When we rest in original blessing, we recognize we are kept by God, seen by God, and given peace by God.

Original Blessing Is Grounded in God

If you haven't noticed, original blessing isn't based on human action or some idealistic view of human perfection. It's founded on trust in God. So when we go looking for proof of original blessing, we don't look to ourselves. We look to God. That's why, when someone asks me how I can believe in original blessing if I'm paying attention to all the problems in the world, I can say it's really beside the point. God has chosen to be faithful to us. That doesn't mean God is always pleased with the way things are going. It just means God's love is bigger. Original blessing is about who God is before it's about who we are and who we're becoming. It is the way God opens up space for us to dwell in God's own goodness. And sure, we are also surrounded by brokenness and sin. But God has made a sovereign choice to be in relationship with us. God has chosen to stick with it. If we reject that, we end up belittling our own relationship to God. If we want to respond gratefully to original blessing, we don't begin by saying, "But . . ." but "Thank you." When we rest in blessing, God's love for us can calm us even in the midst of the mightiest storm.

Because original blessing is grounded in God, it's not some shallow declaration of self-esteem. When everyone gets a trophy, it feels dishonest because the terms of the trophy are different. Not every child has the same athletic ability, or spelling acumen. To treat everyone the same based on a specific criterion feels like a gimmick. But original blessing doesn't tell us we are the same, or that we have equal gifts or talents. It tells us we are all loved, because God freely chooses to look upon us with love. Original blessing is a posture of humility. It's not a reward. It's our identity.

Because original blessing doesn't really have anything to do with our actions, or even our inborn traits, it is the great

17

leveler. We are just as blessed as a Pulitzer prize winner, and just as blessed as a high school dropout. A number of theologians have argued that sin is the great leveler because it equalizes all of us. As Paul said, all have sinned and fall short of the glory of God (Romans 3:23). And it's true, we hold that in common. But we could also say (and I think it's more reverent to God to say) that all have been blessed by God. We hold that in common long before any of us could sin. We are all tethered to God in the same love. So we accept this love only in humility, realizing we share this love and don't own it, and we certainly can't keep it from others. We are recipients of original blessing not because we are special, but because we are human.

So original blessing is not self-righteous. It's not prideful or vain. If we feel confident in ourselves because we are resting in original blessing, that's a good thing! A healthy self-esteem is not at odds with Christian virtues or faithfulness. In fact, it's just the opposite. When our self-esteem reflects God's love for us, we are in sync with God, not in rebellion against God. We will find we are more comfortable in our own skin the more we rest in God's steadfast love for us. Original blessing isn't an overblown sense of self. It's a *natural* sense of self, capable of reflecting on both our strengths and our flaws. Original blessing grounds us in a life with God, and in that grounding, we become at home in our own bodies and our wider world. We have to get rid of the idea that to be God-centered is to denigrate the self. When we are truly God-centered, our humanity becomes beautiful, not insignificant.

When we live into original blessing, we feel a deep sense of self-worth and dignity.

There's one last thing we should know about original blessing being grounded in God: we are not in control of it. We've been given freedom by God to respond to blessing in our own time and in our own way. But there's one place God draws the line on our freedom and says, "Here and no further." We can choose to distance ourselves, dissociate from it, cover it up, bury it, reject it, diminish it, and distort it. But I do not believe God has given us the power to destroy it. We can choose not to echo the blessing of God, but God's blessing will never stop echoing over us. When Paul said that nothing can separate us from the love of God, not life or death, not height or depth, not things present or things to come, he was speaking of the love that is at the heart of original blessing. The gift of love we are given by God is postmarked "Cannot Return to Sender." It is ours to do with what we choose. But the one thing we cannot choose is to destroy it. Because it is not ours to earn, it is not ours to lose either.

Only God can choose to remove original blessing, and God has never revoked it. Even in the most troublesome passages of scripture, God does not renounce blessing. God is sticking with us. There may be hard times, and there may be consequences, but God never says we lost our original goodness. *We* have claimed that. But God never has.

Three Reactions to Blessing

When people encounter the idea of original blessing, they tend to have three basic reactions: relief, anger, and/or fear. For some, accepting that the love God has for them is unchangeable and eternal is joyous relief, like water running over their parched hearts. My friend Laura told me a story of someone who, when hearing about original blessing, wrote in her journal three words, over and over: "I knew it, I knew it, I knew it." Original blessing is a deep truth some were too afraid to believe before, but when they give themselves permission to feel the centered gravity of the love of God anchored in their heart, they recognize it as having been there all along. It is not a rebirth, so much as a home-coming. And it is good to be home. It is a relief.

For some, though, God's insistence to love us without our consent can be infuriating, even insulting. What if I don't believe in God? What if I don't want to follow God? What if I didn't ask God to love me? Those are valid and understandable reactions, but we actually have no control over anyone who loves us, God or otherwise. We can choose how to respond, but we cannot demand that someone stop loving us. It is not our choice to make. You can choose to reject original blessing, and even the notion of God entirely. But if it happens to be true that God is the creator of life and God has chosen to love you as part of that creation, even your rejection of God won't change God's blessing.

For still others, original blessing brings up feelings of fear. Believing in original blessing asks a lot of us, and it can be uncomfortable. We are so steeped in a world that asks us to doubt ourselves, to undermine our own intuition, to belittle our own bodies. Commercials and ads tell us this and, perhaps just as often, we are told this in our churches. It is a constant act of courage and defiance to believe instead that we are beloved. I wish it were easy, because original blessing is the most natural thing. But it can take a very long time to believe in original blessing if we have been told otherwise all our lives. It takes practice, and quite a bit of resilience to block out the yammering chorus of inadequacy that often resides deep within us. It can be scary, when we have become so used to identities built on shame.

It can also be scary because original blessing is incredibly freeing, and with that freedom also comes responsibility. What do we do without a sin nature to justify our choices? To accept the capacity of God to love us no matter what is also to accept our capacity for far greater things than we may have imagined. Scripture echoes this when Romans 8:31 says, "If God is for us, who can be against us?" To be tethered and centered in the power of the unshakeable love of God is to be unleashed in the world as power and light. It can feel both awesome and terrifying. Marianne Williamson wrote,

> Our deepest fear is that we are powerful beyond measure. It is our light, not our darkness that most frightens us. We ask ourselves, Who am I to be brilliant, gorgeous, talented, fabulous? Actually, who are you not to be? You are a child of God. Your playing small does not serve the world. There is nothing enlightened about shrinking so that other people won't feel insecure around you. We are all meant to shine, as children do. We were born to make manifest the glory of God that is

within us. It's not just in some of us; it's in everyone. And as we let our own light shine, we unconsciously give other people permission to do the same. As we are liberated from our own fear, our presence automatically liberates others.[2]

It is not easy to believe in original blessing. The reason we believe so easily in original sin is because it gives us a way to justify and make sense of our disappointments, our own failings and the failings of others, and the deep brokenness of the world. All of this brokenness is overwhelming, and we turn to original sin as if to say, "See! This explains it." But even if original sin explains it (and I don't believe it does), it cannot provide a way out of it. It produces only despair.

And original sin does not, in fact, explain the brokenness of the world. The pain and suffering we experience cannot be absolved by explanation. We do not feel stronger in the face of anguish because of a flow chart. If we say original sin explains the very deep pains in our own lives and in our world, we not only deceive ourselves, but we diminish the truth of our own pain. Suffering is incomprehensible. No explanation can help, ultimately. The only thing that can help is love, and grace, and togetherness. God blesses us with these in the act of original blessing, where we are anointed a dignity that cannot be erased and a solidarity with God that cannot be undone. When we are in the trenches of pain, we cannot always say that God fixes it. But we can say God is with us.

---

2. Marianne Williamson, *A Return to Love: Reflections on the Principles of "A Course in Miracles"* (New York: HarperCollins, 1992).

Choosing Blessing

When we choose to live into our original blessing, we profess that God's love is the most powerful force in the universe, and also that we have no control over it. It's often difficult for us to believe we are loved so unconditionally. It is also difficult to believe that others are beloved. Seeing others' flaws is far more convenient and comfortable, and it doesn't require anything of us but judgment, which we're more than willing to offer. When we say yes to original blessing, we also say yes to our connection with all of creation, and that has considerable effects on the way we live our lives.

Blessing is an overflowing gift, but nothing in this world comes for free. The cost of blessing is to see the world the way God sees the world. In America, we falsely believe freedom means not having to answer to anyone. But freedom in God requires us to be committed not only to God but to each other. While society may tell us to stand alone to be free, God says we can only be free when we stand together. So while we're given a blessing that God chooses not to revoke no matter what, it doesn't mean God has no opinion about what we do with it. God has not created the world to be some sort of divine blessing free-for-all, where there are no consequences and no hardships and no complications, and an endless supply of get-out-of-jail-free cards. We live in a world of natural consequences. If we are destructive in our actions, our relationships, or our words, we cannot expect it to produce life-giving results. That isn't a relationship with God. That's extortion.

I believe God has designed us to live in harmony with God, with each other, and with all of creation. I believe the world is designed to work when we work together, and when we choose to do otherwise, the world suffers, and we suffer, and God suffers. The natural state of affairs is not meant to be brokenness and discord. But we are also free to choose how we respond to God. And our choices matter.

When we choose blessing, we try to live into the way of God in the world. That does require something of us, but it gives us so much more. In a word, it gives us life. We are most alive to God, ourselves, and others when we live a life of blessing. In blessing you receive your deepest identity: God has called you a beloved, blessed child of God. That is the core of who you are. Original blessing means realizing your sin is not the most important thing about you, even if the world—or the church—makes you feel like it is.

God has designed you to live in harmony with God and with others, so that your life may reflect the abundance of the God who created all. When you accept this deep and precious gift, blessedness allows you to rest in the active grace of God, which will forever go before you, around you, behind you, above you, and below you. Blessing allows you to look at the brokenness of the world (and within yourself) with grace and loving-kindness, rather than with shame, hostility, or despair. In blessing you find your calling and purpose, and in blessing you find an unshakeable home in God.

Original Sin is Unnecessary and Unhelpful

We can breathe a big sigh of relief that rejecting the doctrine of original sin is not unorthodox. Well, it is if you use the word "unorthodox" to describe something contrary to the usual or accepted way of seeing something. But if you're using it to label whether something is faithful to our most basic Christian beliefs, then it isn't. "Jesus is Lord" is our most central confession. "I am born with a sin nature" is not.

Since most of us have grown up with a version of Christianity where original sin was assumed, you may be surprised to learn the church flourished for four centuries without any concept of original sin at all. And if we look to the Apostles' Creed and the Nicene Creed, the earliest affirmations of Christian faith, nothing points to belief in an inborn, fallen state of humanity.

Of the three Abrahamic religions, only Christianity has a doctrine of original sin, and Christianity has never held this doctrine universally. Though it may seem that original sin is a given, Christian history tells us a different story. None of the Eastern branches of our family tree (Eastern Orthodox,

Greek Orthodox, Armenian Christian) have ever accepted it, and of course our Jewish forebears, without whom we would not have our tradition, have roundly and consistently rejected it. So Jesus wasn't raised with our notion of original sin, and his disciples wouldn't have been either, or Paul. When they talk about sin in scripture, we would be wise to remember that they don't speak from a Western, developed, or assumed understanding of a sin nature. So we should be mindful to read what they are saying, instead of reading them as if we already know what they mean.

While it's definitely true that the doctrine of original sin is intertwined with a good portion of the rest of Christian theology, it doesn't have to be. And moreover, it shouldn't be. Original sin is the red sock in our theological laundry. It has the potential to discolor everything, and it often does. Moving toward original blessing isn't a move away from orthodox Christian tradition. In fact, I'd argue it may bring us back to some precious gifts we lost along the way.

What Is Original Sin?

Here's what I discovered while working on this book: most everyone thinks they know what original sin is, but the answers widely—and wildly—vary. Most people hold onto a vague notion that original sin is simply the confession that people are not perfect, that we all sin. But if that's all original sin said, I'd hardly need to write a book against it. I'd be the first to agree that nobody is perfect, and I've yet to find anyone who would argue the contrary. We don't need a doctrine to state the obvious. So what is it, anyway?

In its most basic terms, the doctrine of original sin argues two things: one, that when Adam and Eve ate the fruit in the Garden, something negatively and permanently shifted in their nature, and two, this nature has been passed on to every human being since. This sin nature is described in a number of different ways across denominations, but the themes are consistent. Catholics say we "lost our original holiness and justice."[1] Methodists say we are "inclined to evil continually."[2] The Westminster Larger Catechism, used by Presbyterians and other Reformed denominations, says we are "made opposite unto all that is spiritually good, and wholly inclined to all evil, and that continually."[3] National Baptists say our nature is "positively inclined to evil."[4] The prize goes to the Lutheran Book of Concord though, which not only states that original sin is the "entire absence of all good" but also that original sin gives us "a deep, wicked, horrible, fathomless, inscrutable, and unspeakable corruption of the entire nature and all its powers."[5] Yikes.

So the doctrine of original sin is not simply a confession of sin. It is a declaration that human nature is predisposed toward sin. If you imagine a scale of being predisposed toward good on one side and predisposed toward sin on the

1. Catechism of the Catholic Church, Section 404, Paragraph 7 The Fall.
2. Article VII, Articles of Religion, United Methodist Church.
3. Westminster Larger Catechism, Q25.
4. Article III, Articles of Faith, National Baptist Convention, USA.
5. Article 11, Section 1, The Solid Declaration of the Formula of Concord, The Book of Concord.

other, the doctrine of original sin says the scale is weighted toward sin. And because it says that, it implies (when it doesn't state outright) that the goodness with which God blessed creation in Genesis 1 is no longer the most powerful, primary, or central part of our nature. Everyone agrees we retained the image of God. But proponents of the doctrine of original sin believe we lost something in the garden, and it was replaced with something sinful and corrupt. Beyond declaring that all have sinned and fall short of God's glory, the doctrine uses negative totalizing language to describe human nature and our relationship (or tattered remnant of relationship) to God. I find this language dangerous and problematic, and I remain unconvinced that it's necessary. Why can't we just say what the verse itself says? All have sinned and fall short of God's glory. We can leave it at that.

Most theologians tend to want to describe, find answers, and posit reasons for every last thing. You've probably heard the jokes about how many angels can dance on the head of a pin. At some point, though, specificity is not only unnecessary but unhelpful, if only because in theology there is simply no way we'll ever have all the answers. The secret is knowing when you've said all you need, and refusing to say anything beyond it.

When it comes to sin, we can say quite simply that we're human, and humanity carries potential for both good and evil. Any rational conversation we have about human nature will cover all we need to know, including an honest look at sin, without the host of problems and questions the doctrine of original sin brings with it. After all, the man and the woman in the garden of Eden didn't have a sin nature, and they sinned. Why can't we just say the same is true for us?

Original Sin Doesn't Add Up

I know the world has significant problems. But if the doctrine of original sin is true as described above, the world would be rampant with evil, to the point of overflowing. If we are inclined to evil continually, and we have nothing in our human nature to keep us naturally honest or good, then every single person's actions would be more negative than positive, every single day. Is that really the case? Think about your own life. No doubt you have your moments, but do you really feel like you are pushing against some deep inclination to do the wrong thing all the time in all situations?

Or, think of the worst person you know. (Go ahead. They won't have any idea you're thinking of them.) Can you really say that person has never shown any sign of goodness? And even if you claim to know the world's actual worst person, do you really believe that person is the rule and not the exception?

People aren't perfect, but the opposite is also true. People aren't entirely evil. As a matter of perspective, consider the statistics: In 2015, there were 1,165,383 violent crimes in the United States. I wish our crime rate was at zero, and in no way do I want to minimize those sobering numbers. But statistics tend to emphasize only one side. When we look at the total population of the U.S., we come up with its mirror statistic. Of the 320 million people, 318,834,617 of them did not commit a violent crime. There are people every day who steal, attack, lie, swindle, rob, and murder. But for each of those people, there are literally millions more who don't.

I'm not trying to deemphasize all the very real problems we face in the world because of our choices. But I think it's important for us to have some perspective, too, on how overly focused we have become on such a harrowing view of human nature. From a strict numbers perspective, the notion of a whole world of people literally hell-bent on doing evil doesn't add up. And even if it did, I don't see any biblical way around confessing that even the most horrific person still bears the image of God. I may not like it (and often I don't), but we are all God's children.

We Are Not Limited to Two Options

I continually come across the assumption that there are only two options available to us: we believe in original sin, or we believe in some idealistic view of humanity as perfect, or at least capable of being perfect. But these are not the only options. We aren't forced into some "people are evil" vs. "people are perfect" binary. Neither of these extremes are helpful (extremes rarely are), much less realistic, because they are deeply at odds with our own experience of the world. The most honest thing we can say is that people can be good, and people can be evil. They can often be both in the same day, even the same hour. It's problematic to categorize people as entirely one or the other, and also a little naïve. Even a criminal has loved ones; even a saint has skeletons. As with many things, human nature is not an either/or, but a both/ and.

For years, I have followed the work of Cheryl Lawrie, a minister in the Uniting Church of Australia who has led worship in a prison for a number of years. She writes beautiful, vulnerable, honest liturgy and poetry that somehow both name the darkness and shine light upon it at the same time. As someone whose church exists in the walls of a prison, she has a particularly compelling perspective on the complexity of human nature. She writes, "One of the great gifts that working in the prison gave me was the demand to learn to live with complexity. The oh-so-human tendency to categorize people in terms of oppositional binaries—labelling one as good, and the other as bad; one as right, the other as wrong; one as evil and the other as virtuous—falls apart when you sit across the table from someone who has done unspeakable horror, and yet who shows exquisite gentleness in the way they treat a fellow prisoner with mental illness."[6] When we expect people to be entirely good, we are disappointed. When we expect people to be entirely bad, we are humbled. Extremes of both good and evil are too costly to bear.

It's just not true that the only way to take sin seriously is to believe in a doctrine that tells us we are irrevocably flawed. Original blessing doesn't require us to see the world with rose-colored glasses. We don't need to discount the very real brokenness and evil we see and experience in order to affirm

6. Cheryl Lawrie, "All of Who We Are." Web log post. *Holdthisspace.org.au*. N.p., September 30, 2015. Web.

it. It just means we don't confuse the prevalence of sin in the world with a predominance of sin in our nature. What I mean is, just because there are a lot of problems in the world, it does not necessarily follow that we are born with a nature contrary to God and prone to sin. You don't have to look at sin in the world and say, "See? Sin nature!" You can also choose to look at sin in the world and say, "Huh. Humanity."

We are not born innocent, since we are born into a conflicted world. But we are not born sinful, either. We're born human, and within us lies the potential for both creation and destruction, both blessing and curse. To be human is to be capable of both incredible good and terrifying evil. If we deny either side of that potential, we're living unaware. But I believe focusing on our potential for evil as in any way *primary* is unChristian, untrue, and unhelpful. Sin is not the primary thing that is true about us. Before we are anything else, we are made in God's image, and we are made to reflect that image in the way we live. Before scripture tells us anything else about ourselves, it tells us we are good. I think that's because that's the way God intended it. When we ground ourselves in the fact that God created us good, we are capable of confronting all the other things that are true about us, even the difficult things. Love is tremendously healing.

We live in a world where good and evil are all too often intertwined, not only in the world but also in us. What do we do in the face of that? How do we find our way forward? Original blessing is the stubborn assertion not that we are perfect, but that we are loved. And this love has the power to transform even our shadows into light.

****

So, here's the problem. Even though the doctrine of original sin isn't a central tenet of the Christian faith, it IS a doctrine that is widely believed. And it's one that affects absolutely everything else, because it goes to the very heart of how we see ourselves and our relationship with God. And its theology can be harmful, and even damaging or destructive. Why would we believe something so detrimental when it's not even a necessary part of our faith?

Though I find it problematic on a number of levels, I'll just mention four.

Why Wage Unnecessary War with God?

When I had toddlers, I would often call my mom for advice. I had no idea how to handle a two-year-old who wanted to run the entire universe. Though she would give me great specific and practical advice, the most helpful piece of advice is one I've tried to use every day since. She said, "Honey, remember, you guys are on the same team. So don't let them make it a battle. Sit down next to them, and see how you can go forward together." She sure didn't mean that I was supposed to let my toddler run my universe. Usually the way forward included my parental gentle reminder, "Sweetheart, you can't do that." But when my little chubby-cheeked wannabe world dictators were demanding something, I didn't have to see myself standing against them, but beside them in love. It's amazing how that changes the dynamics of your whole relationship, not to mention your response.

Original sin sets up our relationship with God as a battle, because it immediately describes our natures as set against God. It's incredibly harmful for us to describe our relationship with God in negative terms.

If we were to do this with any other major relationship in our lives, it would seem preposterous and even unkind. Nobody looks at a mother who has just given birth and says, "You and your baby do not share all the same genetic markers. You are really not very much alike, when it all comes down to it. There will always be distance between you and your baby, because you are not the same people." No; we celebrate the connection between the two. We revere the bond of life that holds them together, even after the umbilical cord has been cut. Have you ever been to a wedding ceremony where the minister began by describing all the ways the two people are completely incompatible and dissimilar? Of course not. (Or, at least, I hope not.) Or, if someone asked you to describe your best friend, would you ever think to start off with his biggest flaws? Absolutely not.

We describe our most precious relationships in terms of intimacy and connection. We talk about knowing and being known. In healthy relationships, we focus on the good more than we do the not-so-good. Relationship expert John Gottman[7] says he can tell whether a couple is going to last in a marriage after five minutes. Much of it has to do with how they perceive and receive one another. Are they looking for the good, or are they set in what he calls "negative sentiment

---

7. John Mordechai Gottman and Nan Silver, *The Seven Principles for Making Marriage Work* (New York: Crown, 1999).

override"? I think a lot of people are stuck in negative sentiment override with God. They assume God thinks a certain way about them, or is judging them, or rejecting them, or sees them as a failure. And this not only affects the way they feel about themselves, but also how they feel about God. They become defensive, and sometimes angry. Sometimes, they simply accept this feeling of divine rejection because they believe it is the nature of God, which is the most tragic of all. Negative sentiment override can keep us from seeing the good in others, and in ourselves, too.

So one of the most disturbing things about original sin is that it ensnares us in an endless cycle of battle. It is a tour of shame (not duty) that runs on constant redeployment. It hollers at us that we are at war with God, at war within ourselves, at war with the world. We must be on guard, and distrust everything. We are fighting for a peace treaty that will never be signed, because we have already refused the terms of the deal. God has offered us peace, and we have rejected it, choosing instead to clench our teeth and live as bitter soldiers fighting an unstoppable enemy. We cannot find peace in such frenzy. We can only find tired arms, and bloodied fists, and battered, war-torn hearts.

Certainly, there are times when we are indeed at war with God. But even when we are at war with God, God is not at war with us. God is not against us, God is with us. God sits beside us, ready to move us forward together. This is true even in judgment. It is a sign of love and commitment that God will not leave us to our own devices. Sometimes God might say to us, "Sweetheart, you can't do that," but it's always from a place of love, and not from a God who stands against us across the room. God seeks reconciliation in all things, including our own waged wars against God. God wants us to come home. So though we have times when we work against the movement of God in the world, we do not have to be perpetually bitter soldiers. We are not required to enlist. We can set down our arms and choose peace.

When we live into our original blessing, we renounce the endless fighting stance of original sin and choose instead to live with God. We choose to remember that God surrounds us, and sits beside us. We remember that God's relationship to us is not in question. We don't have to live in negative sentiment override. We live in blessing, which overrides even our own rebellion against God.

We define our most cherished relationships in positive and even gracious terms. If we cherish our relationship with God, we should do the same.

The Danger of a Sin Nature

In the same way that it's harmful to describe our relationship with God in negative terms, it's also unhelpful to describe our own nature in negative terms. And that phrase, sin nature, is at the heart of why the doctrine of original sin is so problematic. When we profess to have a sin nature, we're claiming that following God is unnatural. Following God would require us to go against our basic inclinations in order to do what God asks of us. But that creates all kinds of questions. Is it fair for God to ask us to do something we can't do? If we can't do it, are we really guilty? What about the people who do seem to follow God well? Are they only faithful in some way that is outside of their own nature? What does that mean for our understanding of incarnation, and our understanding of Jesus? How can we preach the gospel, or call people to discipleship, if we really think none of us are up to the task? If humanity is really incapable of doing good, what is the point of life, anyway? Why did God create all of us and all of this in the first place?

Of course, most of us don't really approach our faith this way, which is encouraging. But it speaks to the problem of language we have around sin, where throwing around phrases like sin nature can cause a lot of unintended assumptions. If we simply replace sin nature with human nature, we find ourselves in much less complicated space. We can recognize our human ability to follow God faithfully, while also acknowledging that we sometimes go against God in our own lives. And we don't have to describe following God as something that happens outside of ourselves, which is rife with philosophical conundrums. As people who follow an embodied Savior, we can say that we live into the image of God within us, as well as the image of Christ that goes before us. Though neither the image of God nor the image of Christ is owned by us, or contained within us, they are not outside of us, either.

Following God is often difficult, but it is not unnatural. In James 4, James asks, "Do you suppose that it is for nothing that scripture says 'God yearns jealously for the spirit that he has made to dwell in us'?" Our spirit, the soul-life God has given us, is meant to indwell with God. When we choose anything else, God doesn't say, "It figures. That's their nature, after all." God is jealous, and yearns for us to return to our intended path. Our love has a home, and it is not with the ways that go against God in the world, but the way of God in the world. It is with life, and not death; it is with love, and not destruction. James then tells us to draw near to God, and God will draw near to us. When we leave, as we surely will, we only have to return, and we will find God waiting. God is sitting beside us, not fighting us from across the room.

The nature of God is faithfulness and steadfast love. Our human nature is intended to embody that same love and faithfulness in response to God. And when we do, we don't go against our nature, or do so from somewhere outside of ourselves. We do it as human beings made in the image of God, called to follow God with our whole selves. We do it as people grounded in original blessing. We do it as people who are working with our nature, not against it.

Protecting Personhood

I'm also wary of the idea of a sin nature because it devalues humanity. I don't mean that we ought to put humanity on a pedestal, but there's a direct correlation between how we value something and how we treat it. If we see someone doing something wrong, original sin gives us an easy way to categorize him as evil. And if we feel justified in calling someone evil, or even bad, we tend to use very different criteria in the way we treat them. We lose our Christian conviction in that moment, because we no longer seek to serve the other, much less love the other. Seeing people as inherently flawed is a terribly convenient way to devalue each other, even if that isn't what the doctrine intended.

I once heard award-winning broadcast journalist and producer Soledad O'Brien describe how race became a social construct.[8] Race isn't really a thing, after all, unless you're talking about the human race. So how did it become such a potent and destructive belief? After poring over thousands of pages of European explorers' travel journals to Africa, O'Brien was pleasantly surprised to see that all of the references to the African people were laudatory. That is, until the fifteenth century, when language became not only negative but downright condemning. The same people who a generation before were hailed as kings and leaders and innovators were now being called beasts and savages. What happened? In a word, phenotypes. Phenotypes are a form of classification used to split up the human race into separate categories. So, instead of recognizing tensions between groups as a matter of clan rivalry or socio-economic factors, phenotype classification dissected the actual human race into separate groups. The problem, of course, is that the minute you separate people out into groups, you set them against one another.

When people began using phenotype classification, race became seen as an inborn trait. It changed perception from "he looks different" to "he is different." Soon, these differences

8. Soledad O'Brien, "Race in America." www.Qideas.org. Q Commons, 20 Apr. 2015. http://qideas.org/videos/race-in-america/.

in physical appearance carried the false perception of other traits with them: intellect, moral aptitude, strength. And, because these traits were perceived as inborn, people began to accept the idea that some humans were born superior to others. Not surprisingly, when colonialists began engaging in slave trade in their quest for Euro-Western dominance, phenotypical classification proved to be a helpful tool to justify their actions. Years later, it would be the foundational assumption in Hitler's quest for a perfect race. It's the reason American history contains a 3/5 compromise. The invention of phenotype classification paved the way for racism, ethnic cleansing, apartheid, and a whole host of other destructive beliefs to take hold.

The whole global human community has suffered so much destruction because of that one false shift in perception. It's a reminder how much our beliefs and perceptions matter.

Even in its most benign forms, classifying people by their nature leads to a problematic hierarchy of desirables vs. second-class citizens. Whether it's race, gender, age, sexual orientation, physical appearance, citizenship status, or any number of other possibilities, categorizing people nearly always leads to oppression by the majority in power. Categorizing is never far from minimizing. It is a dangerous endeavor.

Categorizing people with a sin nature minimizes the image of God in each of us. A sin nature advocates for something like a lowest common denominator. Nobody benefits by sinking down like that. And history tells us that those with the least power will be hurt by that system most of all.

I'm also bothered by the idea that asserting someone's sinful nature can be a dangerous justification for punishment. When you consider every kind of abuse, every one of them began with an attack on a person's inherent worth. Targeting self-esteem is an easy way to get power over someone. Cult leaders, abusive parents, manipulative authority figures, and disgraceful religious leaders all prey on a person by insisting she cannot have opinions, his viewpoint doesn't count, they deserve whatever happens to them. On behalf of battered women, abused children, and manipulated cult members who have suffered at the hands of wrongful power, we should adamantly refuse to consider any sort of belief that requires us to devalue ourselves.

Especially in a world that seems more and more prone to religious extremism, I believe it's both healthy and necessary to be resistant to any religion or belief that requires someone to deny her personhood. As Christians, we are called to fight injustice, protect the orphan and the widow, and consider others as better than ourselves. When we look at the stories of Jesus, we see someone who brought dignity to outcasts and restored humanity to those forgotten or despised. God never asks us to reject our human dignity. God calls us to live into it.

When we live by original blessing, we have no excuse to treat others poorly. We are called instead to see everyone as bearers of God's image, and therefore creatures of inherent worth and dignity. And it then becomes our responsibility to respect and uphold their dignity as well as our own.

Original Sin: A Theological Extreme Makeover

Like seemingly every other American, I do love a good makeover show. There's something fulfilling about seeing change happen so quickly, probably because in our own lives it usually happens at tortoise-like pace. But I'm not in favor of theological extreme makeovers, where we pit God and humanity against one another just so we can create a more dramatic happy ending. And there's something a little too "evangelical youth camp" to me about the dramatic narrative of original sin.

If you've ever known anyone who has been on a makeover show or even reality television, you know that what we see is dramatically staged and exaggerated. "Before" pictures are made to look as frumpy or run down as possible, and "after" pictures are given optimal lighting and effects, as well as extra props. The result is satisfying, but it's not entirely honest. And it gives us false perceptions about what we should expect or experience in our own lives, which seem humdrum by comparison.

My grandmother loves romance novels and reads them voraciously, so I often take her to the bookstore to load up on ten or twenty at a time. (I say that to explain to you how many back flaps of western romance novels I have had the occasion to read, which is a lot.) Every last one of them is the same: Jimmy Cowboy has spent his life building fences around his heart, until one day Shayna comes along. They hate each other. Their families/best friends/rival oil companies have longstanding hostility toward one another.

But then sparks fly between the two of them. Will they ever find the courage to give in to this love? I've yet to see a plot synopsis about two well-adjusted people who hit it off and decide to spend life together. The whole romance paperback industry runs on drama and conflict. It's "I hate you! I love you! Oh, Jimmy!" all the way.

While that's just the way things go on home makeover shows, reality TV, and romance paperbacks, when it comes to talking about God, I prefer honesty over dramatic staging. I think it shows a profound lack of trust when we feel the need to dress up God, or Jesus, or the gospel, or faith in general, in dramatic and conflicting terms. Life has enough drama on its own, and so does scripture. We don't need to invent it, or overemphasize it.

I wonder if this is one of the reasons people so willingly believe in original sin. The conflict between humans as so bad and God as so good is narratively appealing. And for some Christians, the entire gospel is centered around the idea of a kind of Salvation Extreme Makeover, where a person goes from irreparably sinful to eternally saved with one short prayer or in one single moment. Sometimes salvation does happen like that, and that's wonderful. But the idea that every person's salvation story *needs* that same level of drama to be real or true is unrealistic, and a little immature.

That extreme narrative can also be shameful and detrimental. Spiritual abuse can come at the hands of others, but it's also something we can inflict upon ourselves. For some, the extreme distance between themselves and God is so great, they have to use damaging language to describe themselves (I'm worthless to God, I'm nothing but a pile of rags, I'm a worm) or worse, use damaging action against themselves. There is nothing of God in such an act. That's not faithful, but harmful.

I've lost count of how many times I've read that original sin is an effective bonding agent between humans, like we're all members of the same classroom detention. We need it because it keeps us together as a shared universal experience. That sounds like dramatic staging to me. And while it's true that we bond over difficulty, it's also true that we bond over celebration, joy, and shared happiness. Because what bonds us together is love, and more specifically the love of God, which has room for both grief and delight.

Many proponents of original sin say it's the only way for us to understand how much we rely on grace. I don't think that's true, and I also think that's dangerous. God's grace can't and shouldn't be twisted and used as a way for us to feel like we're unworthy. God doesn't need to humiliate us before giving us grace just to ensure the grace is effective and appreciated. If God set up the world to work that way, we would all be suffering from grace-induced PTSD. God wouldn't be any different than an abusive parent who, before harming a child, says "It's for the best." I profoundly reject a god like that. If we are told we have to feel bad before we can appreciate feeling loved, it isn't love we've found.

The spiritual life can be thrilling, and life with God can have moments in ALL CAPS. But much of our spiritual life won't be that way, and that doesn't make it any less real or true. We know we can get addicted to the thrill of the extreme makeover, the rush of someone going from drab to fab, or a house going from ho-hum to hello! But a deeply satisfying relationship with God doesn't require flashing lights and reality TV drama. When we get to know God, we can see grace in even the smallest things. We can hear God not only in a shout, but also a whisper.

When I was a pastor, a family with kids came to visit our church one Sunday. They wanted to know what our vision for kids was and how we were going to "make kids fall in love with Jesus." I smiled and admitted I have no control over whether anyone falls in love with Jesus, but that our intention was to help them get to know Jesus, and trust that he is compelling enough on his own. I explained that our church wasn't the kind of place that was going to use a lot of incentives like toys or candy to teach about Jesus. We trust the kids will like him without all of that.

It's tough to trust the basics in a society so addicted to drama. When we live in a culture where even our shampoo is enhanced (50 percent more shine!), we eventually lose our ability to see the natural world as something remarkable all on its own. As we look to God, I hope we don't make the same mistake.

God is beautiful, as is. Jesus is compelling, as is. The gospel is good news, and good-enough news, for goodness sake, as is. Grace is beautiful, as is.

Instead of feeling we need to create an extreme makeover, maybe we can learn to trust that God is enough.

It might help if we begin by remembering our blessing, where God tells us we are loved, we are enough, *as is*.

A Tale of Two Boxes and a Golden Thread

When we look at Christian history, it's best to remember that it's made up of people trying to figure out what it means to follow Jesus, just like you and me. And generally, they did so with really good intentions, and often under difficult circumstances. Especially at the beginning of Christianity, so many groups were trying to make their version of the Jesus story the only one, and we owe much to the leaders who staunchly kept the basic story intact. We're here because of their faithfulness.

As that story has been carried from generation to generation for two thousand years, we've had a good deal of time to debate the particulars. And we should, because it's a sign of our faithfulness. We continually ask what it means to follow Jesus in our time. Sometimes, we look back and learn from our mistakes. As we trace the path of the doctrine of original sin's development, I believe we can honor the Jesus followers who were doing their best to make sense of God in their time, while also questioning and rejecting some of their conclusions along the way.

From Easter to the early church and through the first four hundred years of Christianity, the church experienced remarkable growth and became a steady force for good. In the most critical time in Christian history, where we would either catch on or die out, the gospel caught on. And it did so without any concept of original sin. But by the time we got to the Protestant Reformation in the 1500s, we had moved from being a church that had no doctrine of original sin at all to one that had an entire branch convinced all of humanity was totally depraved. Talk about theological whiplash.

If we want to understand how we ended up here, one very broad way of looking at it is to imagine two boxes. One box is labeled "death," and the other box is labeled "sin." Of course, death and sin are deeply entwined concepts, and both are integral to the story of God. It does us no good to attempt to separate them, and we don't want to disconnect them. But we *do* want to see them in proper perspective. So the question is, is death the bigger reality, or is sin? Picture it this way: Either there is a box labeled "death" and sin is inside the box, or there is a box labeled "sin" with death inside.

For the early church, fresh on the heels of experiencing the risen Christ, the answer was clear. The gospel is a story of life and death. When the disciples share the good news in Acts, those stories reveal a clear pattern of declaring the central truth of Easter: in Jesus, God has triumphed over death. Because of this, we can turn to God for healing and life. As a result of their belief in the power of God over death, the crowds often ask what they should do, and the disciples tell them to repent from their sins and turn to God. It is a call from death to life first, and then as a result of that desire to move toward life, it is a call from sin to forgiveness and redemption. John 3:16, which is so often used as a clarion call to repentance, also speaks in this way. "For God so loved the world that God gave his only Son, so that whoever believes in him *will not perish, but will have everlasting life.*"

When we think of the story of God from start to finish, God continually offers life. Creation is of course one example, but also the rainbow covenant, the exodus, the kings and prophets. Think about it: God redeemed the Israelites out of slavery as a declaration of life, not personal sin forgiveness. And Jesus said, "I am the life," not "I am the forgiveness."

Of course sin and forgiveness of sin come right at the heels of death and life. Where one is, there is the other. But life and death are the big picture. Forgiveness is just one of the many gifts we receive when we have life in God.

So here's the most basic church history lesson I can muster for you: in 1054, the church split, and when they did, they chose different boxes. The East chose death, and the West chose sin. And ever since that fork in the road, Western Christianity has organized its theology around the assumption that sin is the pivotal reality.

The Eastern Church believes the good news is primarily a story about God overcoming *death*. Easter is the celebration of resurrection, and resurrection is God's triumph over death. The Eastern Church's understanding of sin, human nature, the sacraments, and the mission of the church all preserve an emphasis on resurrected life as God's answer to death, not sin. Maybe this is why nobody uses the term Orthodox guilt. It's definitely why the Eastern Orthodox church does Easter like nobody else, complete with a marathon from-night-to-the-next-morning worship service. Easter is the biggest deal, the central reality. And it's about life, not just forgiveness of sins.

In contrast, Western Christians began to see sin as the big problem, and sin replaced death as the central focus. What followed was a doctrine of original sin, and all the theological rearrangements that came along with it. If sin is the big problem to fix, then you need a doctrine to describe the big problem, and a doctrine of atonement to describe how the problem of sin is fixed on the cross. And the mission of the church goes from bringing life to the world to getting sinners into heaven. And on and on it goes. This is where the blanket started to go crooked. When we ask how we got here, the theological switch between a focus on death to sin is the first major shift.

Christian faith cannot be boiled down to sin and repentance without losing the depth and beauty of a full relationship with God. God calls us to life, not acquittal. The story of God is so much bigger than our personal faults. The goal isn't just forgiveness, but new creation. It is a matter of life and death, in the widest and deepest possible way.

The Big Picture of Life and Death

Original blessing is a declaration of life. In fact, it's the first gift we receive in life. With our first breath, we are given relationship with the one who created us. As we remember that blessing is both an origin and a goal, a being and a becoming, we see how the themes of life and death continually play out in the biblical story.

In the Hebrew scriptures, the call to choose life comes over and over again. In Deuteronomy 30, Moses gathers together all the Israelites who have traveled through the wilderness for forty years. They gather to renew their covenant with God before they enter into the promised land. Moses takes this moment to remind them that God has freed them from captivity, sustained them in the wilderness, and now sends them forth. Moses says,

> I call heaven and earth to witness against you today that I have set before you life and death, blessings and curses. Choose life so that you and your descendants may live, loving the Lord your God, obeying him, and holding fast to him; for that means life to you and length of days, so that you may live in the land that the Lord swore to give to your ancestors, to Abraham, to Isaac, and to Jacob.[1]

Obviously, Moses isn't telling the people to get up and choose to be alive in the morning. He is telling them to choose a certain way of being alive. Loving God and obeying God means life to us. In our relationship with God, we are grounded in both life and love.

In the New Testament, we see both a continuation and a deepening of this understanding. It is as if Jesus puts a magnifying glass over these choices, so we clearly see the destruction that comes when we choose death, and we see how distinctly and dramatically a person can change by being restored to life through healing and forgiveness. The New

---

1. Deuteronomy 30:19–20 NRSV.

Testament declares that new life begins immediately when a person chooses to walk in the ways of God. We don't have a trial period before we are accepted, and we don't have to prove anything. If we ask, God gives us this new life in a moment. It is ours to have, any time we ask for it, just as our original blessing is always there awaiting our return. Again, we see a pattern of both origin and goal. New life is both something we receive immediately, and something we live into throughout our days.

The disciples in Acts spoke about life most often in this immediate way, because they were encouraging people to move toward new life. But it is important for us to remember that, for them, choosing to follow God was not only or even primarily about life in the hereafter, but about the choices we make for life and in life beginning now. This has always been the emphasis of scripture, from beginning to end. God sets before us life and death, and our calling daily, in all we do, is to choose life.

There is one other way we see life described in the scriptures. We await life in the future, as God brings all things to new creation. Life is not just happening now, and not only happening continually, but also something we live into as we go. If you imagine life as a sphere, the future of life in new creation is a way of moving that sphere beyond the present, so that as we move, we move both toward it and into it. Life is that big. Moving toward life is less of an expectation and more like an orientation. We do not know what new creation will mean, in the particular. We must be brave enough to release ourselves from needing to know or expect anything exact. But when we follow God, we orient ourselves toward the kind of life that is unbounded even by time, even by the cosmos. Life cannot be contained by the past and the present, but must include even that which we cannot yet see. Life is that big. More specifically, life *in God* is that big.

In the same way that life has a broad biblical understanding, death means far more than physical mortal death. It encompasses separation from God, broken relationship, violence, stubbornness, and injustice of every kind. If life is new creation and re-creation, death is degradation and destruction. When Moses stands before the Israelites and tells them to choose life or death, he means for them to choose in each decision and action which direction they want to go. Will you move toward death or toward life?

Scripture echoes this sentiment again and again. In Judges, the refrain *The Israelites did evil in the sight of the Lord* is repeated on what feels like an unending loop. Most of the time, they turn away from the Living God to worship dead idols. They choose the dead over the Living. Then God sends a judge or a leader, and they turn back toward life. But alas, they choose death again, and the cycle repeats. With the choice of death comes war, and pillaging, and other markers of destruction.

We see the same cyclical nature in the books of the prophets as well. The people fall away from choosing life, and God sends a prophet to remind them of the covenant and turn them back. And again, the characteristics of death are everywhere: worshiping false gods, mistreating the poor, ruining the land, forgetting the covenant. All of these choices lead to our demise, both individually and corporately. They degrade our relationship with God, and our relationship to our own selves as God's people and to one another. There's no life in them. The judges and the prophets and the leaders come to turn us away from death and back toward the way of life. So death is far more than something that awaits all of us at the end of our lives. It is something we are up against in every decision we make.

So it may be more accurate (and theologically appropriate) to say we have a death nature, not a sin nature. (But only if you also say we have a life nature!) Death is the Big Bad. It is the primary, primal problem. Jesus died on the cross for your death. Or, Jesus entered death to save you from it. Or, Jesus experienced death so that Jesus could be with you even in the depths of the grave. Because after all, Jesus is the incarnation of God sticking with it.

The Golden Thread of Blessing

In George MacDonald's story, *The Princess and the Goblin,*[2] a young princess lives in a big house in the country. Unbeknownst to her, goblins live in the mountains nearby, and they constantly dig tunnels and create caves in the hopes of drawing nearer to the village and its inhabitants. So the princess is kept hidden safely in the house, where one day she becomes lost and stumbles upon an old woman in the

2. George Macdonald, *The Princess and the Goblin* (N.p.: Rossignol, 2015). Note: This is the only truly unabridged version of the story in print, and I highly recommend this one over the others!

attic, sitting at a spinning wheel with golden thread. She learns this woman is her great great grandmother, who claims to have been there the whole time, watching over her. The grandmother tells her this golden thread is woven into all things, and if the princess will hold onto it, she will always be able to find her way back to her. When goblins tunnel under the country house itself, threatening to flood the princess and everyone else within its walls, the princess follows the golden thread and finds her way to safety. The thread saves her, because it is her connection to life.

When we find our home in original blessing, we tether ourselves to the deepest source of life within us. No matter what comes our way, no matter what goblins seek to tunnel under our house, we can find our way to life when we follow our unbreakable link with God. So blessing isn't just a nice thought, or an interesting idea. It is a matter of life and death. It is the golden thread God gives each of us when God calls us into existence.

When my son was young, he would get a little anxious when I left town, so I would ask him, "Do you want me to tell you about the special red string again?" He would nod his little head and say yes, and I would snuggle up with him in his bed and hold him. I would put my hand on his heart, and he would put his hand on my heart, and I would say, "When you were born, you were connected to me by a cord from my body to yours, and they cut it. But there is another string that still connects us, one they can never cut. It is an invisible red string of love between your heart and my heart. No matter how far I go, it stretches. No matter what you do, it is there. And it will always be with you."

You and I have learned to live independently of our parents, and if we ever needed assurance like that, we don't anymore. But we have too often been told that we live separated from our Divine Parent, and that is not only heartbreaking. It is also a lie. We are not born fallen. We are born tethered to God with golden thread. It is a thread that can never be broken. And that thread will always, always lead us to life.

We are not born fallen—and yet, for many of us, that's the only version we've been told about what happened with Adam and Eve in the Garden of Eden. They ate an apple, and when they did, their relationship with God—and ours with it—was permanently disfigured and disordered. Now instead of a golden thread connecting us to God, there is a chasm of sin separating us from God.

But maybe that isn't the only way to read the story. Maybe we can return to the Garden, and take a second look, and find that even a story about disobedience can end in life.

II. Revisiting the Garden

Let's All Take a Deep Breath about Genesis

One of the biggest mistakes we make when reading scripture is that we come to the text demanding something of it. Don't misunderstand me: scripture has so much to give us, more than we can imagine. But scripture cannot be anything other than what it is. I don't believe the function of scripture is to make us feel better, or to give us an answer, or to tell us what to do. It can do these things, and very often does; but the function of scripture is revelation, certainly of God but also of what we may need to confront, realize, accept, or see differently. When we come to scripture, we do so knowing it will likely demand something of us.

Scripture is a sacred book meant to provoke us in ways that will move us toward God. And often, that is the very last thing we are looking for. We would rather have an answer, a simple plan, even a nicely tidy moral story. But scripture gives us none of these things, because the holy is anything but domestic. We go looking to find a plan and instead are sent on a treasure hunt.

If scripture has any authority at all, it is precisely because it refuses to cower to our demands upon it, even after two thousand years. It remains stubbornly strange and confusing and glorious, even as it is revealing the holy to us through the ineffable ways of the Spirit. If scripture reveals who God is, then we must accept that God remains in many ways unknowable even after thousands of pages. God also refuses to stay trapped in the pages of a book, even a holy one inspired by God's own Spirit. It is incredibly problematic, but that's God for you.

We expect scripture to do things for us it has never promised. We make demands upon the text that it simply isn't willing to meet. And in terms of sheer volume, on a scale of pure expectation, there is perhaps no more loaded passage of scripture than Genesis 3.

So I would like for you to consider whether your expectations of Genesis 3 are not the tiniest bit too ambitious. If the story of Jesus took four gospels and hundreds of chapters to tell (and if you know Jesus at all, you've already realized they hardly contain all you know and feel about him, much less what is actually true of him), then it is presumptuous to expect one chapter in Genesis to tell you everything you need to know about death, sin, human nature, immortality, the laws of the universe, and humankind's struggle. Consider the possibility that while Genesis 3 is a great text to spark questions, it isn't trying to *answer* a good number of those questions. It is not trying to determine how sin entered the world, or where death came from, or why people sin. Genesis 3 is not a laboratory experiment where we get conclusive results about some shocking alteration to our human DNA. If we have sane and simple expectations for the story, we will be much more equipped to read what it says, rather than what we think it means.

That being said, Genesis 3 has wisdom to teach us, deep wisdom that we all too often have overlooked in our search for certainty. And we may find that this little chapter does, in fact, have the capacity to hold a great number of very big questions about life, death, and human existence. But it will only teach them to us on its own terms.

I would also encourage you to see the text literarily. (Did your brain fill in a different word you were expecting?!) By literarily, I mean that you accept the text as what it is, which is a piece of literature. It is holy, inspired literature, but it is literature nonetheless. Genesis 3 is not journalistic live reporting. It is a story passed down through storytelling from one generation to the next, until at last we had the means of writing the story down to preserve for future generations. It has an audience, and a narrator, and primary characters. Because it's good literature, it has a crisis, and a climax, and a resolution, too. Rather than asking the text to be the first, sole, or primary spiritual, philosophical, psychological, and sociological statement about humanity, we could choose instead to accept it as what it is: a story from scripture, meant to provoke us in ways that will move us toward God.

It can far and away exceed that particular expectation.

A Second Look

One of the dangers of discussing a well-known passage of scripture is that we assume we already know what it means. I think of the time when Jesus went home to Nazareth and was unable to do any miracles there, and he remarked that a prophet is never honored in his hometown.[1] When we're too familiar with something, we often lose our ability to see it clearly.

We are all too familiar with Genesis 3. It is iconic, meaning it has transcended even the pages of scripture and is now a cultural artifact. A shiny red apple, for example, immediately brings Genesis 3 to mind, even though the shiny red apple is a feature of the fairy tale of Snow White and not the story of Genesis. (Genesis 3 says fruit, not apple. A fruit from a tree *could* be an apple, but it could also be a pear, or an orange.) So the apple is an appropriate metaphor for what we are dealing with in Genesis 3. We read details into the text that are not there, and we narrow our perception to but one of many possible interpretations. We assume the fruit in the story is an apple, when in reality it could be any number of things. Even the name we have given this story, the fall, shows how powerful our preconceived notions can be. The word "fall" is nowhere in the text. And for us to have fallen, humanity had to have been placed on a pedestal of some kind, right?

So let's talk about three assumptions you may have made about Genesis 3 that are worth reconsidering.

1. Matthew 13:54–58.

First, most people assume the serpent in Genesis 3 is Satan. But scripture doesn't say that. (In fact, much of what Christians assume about Satan comes from sources outside of scripture.) The serpent is identified only with the Hebrew word *arum*. Arum is usually translated crafty or cunning, but it's worth noting that the six other times the word is used, all in Proverbs, it is positive, meaning prudent or sensible. Though I'm not arguing for that particular translation here, it gives us perspective to realize not only that the serpent is not named specifically as Satan but also that his craftiness is not categorically or only evil, either. The word simply doesn't lend itself to that conclusion.

Second, countless theologians have taken the liberty to describe the garden as perfect before the man and the woman ate the fruit. (They aren't given names until after this story, yet another detail we overlook.) Of course, the story itself only describes a fruitful, verdant place, a garden teeming with life. A far better word, if we had to choose, would be harmony or wholeness, which is much more in line with a Hebrew worldview. Perfection carries a lot of baggage with it, particularly about morality, and it stems not from a biblical view of the world but from Greek philosophy.

I think perfection is yet another way we veer toward an extreme theological makeover, where the pristine purity of the garden is pitted against this idea of a despised and worthless ruin afterward. But Genesis never says the whole garden went up in flames, so to speak. If anything, the act of the man and the woman leaving the garden seems to show that the garden is still fully intact. When they eat of the fruit, the story doesn't say the leaves all started dying or the birds fell dead to the ground. The garden went on thriving just as it had before, as far as we know.

Lastly, in no place in Genesis 1–3 does scripture describe the man and the woman as immortal. They are created by God and given life by God, but nothing in the creation stories tell us that death is not present. In fact, everything God created has a natural cycle of life and death—the trees, the flowers, animals and plants, and yes, humanity. Genesis 2:17 says, "Don't eat from the tree of the knowledge of good and evil, because on the day you eat from it, you will die!" It does not say death will enter into the world. The fact that the man and the woman understood what God meant proves that death was a reality they already knew, even if they had not yet experienced it.

These assumed details add much drama to the text of Genesis 3 (Satan! The end of the perfect world! The beginning of death and the end of immortality!), but I wonder if we could trust instead that the text is meaningful enough without our extraneous additions. Again, there's no need to turn this into an extreme makeover. When left with the plain text, we still have more than enough meaning to ponder.

Genesis: The Hebrew Story of Creation

As a pastor I always began speaking about a passage by locating it first. Who wrote this, and when? What was happening? What was going on in the world at that time?

These seem like obvious questions to ask in order to comprehend what it means, but far too often we expect scripture to display a certain kind of timelessness, as if it floats above the fray. But of course, there is a difference between timeless and everlasting, and scripture is more aptly described as everlasting. When we try to make scripture timeless, we find that we have to scrub it of its detail and quirks, of its dates and histories. Scripture is not timeless because it came to us in the midst of human history, shared by breath and voice before it was recorded with paper and ink. These stories were contained in one part of the world before they expanded to reach the rest of the world. Scripture has a rich and complex history, and its pages are marked by the fingerprints and lives of many who lived before us. We can say scripture is everlasting, though, because wherever we are in human history, whatever we are facing, we will find wisdom in its pages. As Solomon said, there is nothing new under the sun, and so we find that the wisdom of God speaks to us across history and time and geography—and it does not need to erase them to do so.

The ancient Near East is filled with creation stories. When I took religion classes in college, I was shocked to learn that Genesis shares a number of common elements with its ancient Near Eastern counterparts. And though as a college freshman these pagan parallels to my beloved scripture were a rattling realization, it didn't take long to realize how different they are despite their surface similarities. Like every other story, Genesis came about in a particular time and place, among particular people. The story is one of flesh and blood, latitude and longitude, culture and symbolism. We can learn from what the Bible has in common with other stories as much as we can learn from the ways they differ.

For one, the Genesis creation story is the only story that is markedly and remarkably nonviolent. In the Babylonian *Enuma Elish*, for instance, the two gods Marduk and Tiamat are locked in fierce battle. When Marduk defeats Tiamat, he splits her body open like a clam and then fashions the world out of her separated body parts. The world literally comes from the bloody spoils of battle. In all the Near Eastern tales, the act of creation is a chaotic one, marked with dissension and rivalry and violence. And the inference is clear: we humans are at their whims. It's a terrifying notion.

In stark contrast, the story of creation in Genesis is not an act of chaos but of harmony. God chooses to make the world with intention. The God of the Bible creates the world in peace, not in conflict, revenge, or bloodshed. Creation is the result not of destruction, but of God's goodness overflowing. Genesis consistently describes a God in control and not in chaos, and presents a world that is designed with an internal order. God looks upon creation and says, "It is very good." It's not a declaration of war victory but a declaration, over and over, of creation's goodness. And perhaps most radical of all, God lives in close relationship to all God has made. Though this seems self-evident to us, it was a radical reorientation for the first hearers of Genesis.

If we imagine creation to be something as simplistic as a utopian happy-go-lucky place where nothing ever will go wrong, we disparage the beauty and harmony illustrated in the Genesis stories. God's goodness is not that shallow and neither is God's creation. I wonder if there is not something immature about our desire for the garden to be perfect. Perfection is, in a sense, very naïve. It's almost as naïve and problematic as believing that one action in Genesis 3 is supposed to upend God's entire created order. These assumptions seem to reject the very sovereignty of God the book of Genesis is trying to show us. In contrast to the other Mesopotamian gods, the God of the Israelites is loving and good and intentional. All of creation finds its meaning within its relation to God.

A more appropriate view of creation would be not perfection but potential. God designed the world to develop and function in a certain way, while allowing for creation to live freely into its potential. Sometimes creation will live up to and into its potential, while other times it will renounce it. Seeing the biblical story as a story of what we do with our God-given potential seems far more honest—both in relation to our lives and in relation to the text itself. Potential reminds us once again that goodness is both an origin and a goal. It is given to us as a gift, but it is also given to us as a calling.

Genesis in the Rest of Scripture

You may be surprised to learn that Genesis 3 is rarely referenced in the rest of scripture. In fact, it isn't mentioned at all in the rest of what is traditionally considered the Old Testament. This should remind us the Genesis 3 story wasn't central to a biblical understanding of sin in humanity for a very long time. Or at least, the story wasn't seen so negatively or centrally that it colored our understanding of everything else. This is yet another example of how our modern assumptions and expectations of Genesis 3 are too high.

The first time it is possibly referenced is in the apocryphal book of Sirach. (The Apocrypha is a collection of books that are included in the Roman Catholic Bible but omitted from the Protestant one.) Sirach 25:24 says, "From a woman sin had its beginning, and because of her we all die." Taken out of context, it sounds like a pretty straightforward indictment of Eve, if not all women. So it's important to note that the following verse commands a husband to refuse his wife water, and in prior verses declares that a man's gloomy face, drooping hands, and weak knees are a result of an evil wife. The entire section reads a bit like an angry letter from a dejected teenage boy, to be honest. In the same way some psalms describe strong emotions without necessarily endorsing them, Sirach seems to display the passionate feelings of a man who feels betrayed. Rather than using this obscure verse to pin all of human sin on Eve, it would be more appropriate to see it as yet another example of how some men sometimes feel about some women when they are angry. Or, to be more charitable, we could see it as an example of how some people tend to overstate things when they are in a huff. In any case, Eve is not mentioned specifically, nor is Genesis, so the reference to women may be more generalized to women as the bearers of human life which will always result in death, rather than a definite allusion to Genesis 3.

The second place we see an allusion to Genesis 3 is in the tenth chapter of the Wisdom of Solomon, also an apocryphal book. Wisdom is used as a metaphorical description of the Spirit.

> Wisdom protected the first-formed father of the world, when
>   he alone had been created;
> she delivered him from his transgression, and gave him strength
>   to rule all things.
> But when an unrighteous man departed from her in his anger,
> he perished because in rage he killed his brother.
> When the earth was flooded because of him, wisdom again
>   saved it,
> steering the righteous man by a paltry piece of wood.

Here, we see Wisdom (Spirit) as protecting the man Adam, delivering him from his transgression, and giving him strength. It's a far more gracious view of Adam than we're used to seeing. Then in the next verse, Cain is called unrighteous because he departed from Wisdom. Murder is described as an act stemming from anger, not some kind of sin nature. In verse 4, the earth is said to have flooded because of man (and the allusion is clearly to the people in Noah's day if we're pointing fingers here, not Adam), but also saved by Wisdom who needed only a "paltry piece of wood" to do so. If anything, these verses provide a measured view of human nature, reinforcing our need to stay close to God (the fount of Wisdom) in order to live into our goodness. We need wisdom. But that doesn't mean we have a sin nature.

If we don't count these two apocryphal mentions (which do not support original sin), the entire traditional Old

Testament does not refer back to Genesis 3. That's pretty remarkable, because the Old Testament is known for its repetitive teaching nature, reminding the people of God again and again of what God has done, of what led them here, of why they should change their ways. For a religion based so strongly on remembrance, it's critically important that they do not take the time to remember Genesis 3 with a ritual, festival, sacrifice, or even a mention in a rousing speech.

When we get to the New Testament, Jesus never mentions Genesis 3. He never mentions Adam, or Eve, or the Garden. Out of the twenty-seven books in the New Testament, there are only three references at all. And you probably know them already, because they've been consistently quoted (and often with far-reaching assumptions) in modern American Christianity.

The first is Romans 5:12–17, where Paul describes sin entering the world through one man, and contrasts the sin of Adam with the righteousness of Christ. Paul describes Adam as a type of the one who was to come. Paul is using Adam here not literally but typologically, as a person who stands for more than just the person. And he says not only that Adam is a type, but that Adam is a type of the one who was to come, who is of course Jesus. If we can talk about the totality of the human experience with Adam, we can also talk about the totality of God's grace with Jesus.

But saying that Adam represents human experience does not equal original sin. Nowhere in these verses does Paul say that we inherited a nature. He says that we all find resonance with the type who is Adam, who is a sinner. None of us would disagree with that. And we wouldn't disagree with his response, either, which is that in Jesus human sin is returned for every type of grace, the free gift offered us. Paul is trying to cast a wide net and put all of humanity in the same boat: we are sinners. And Jesus offers all of us a free gift of abundant grace. That's the gospel. It's not original sin.

The second reference to Adam also comes from Paul, this time in 1 Corinthians 15:21–22. As in Romans, he sets up Adam as a universal type, in order to show Jesus as another universal type. And because here Paul is concerned with explaining the importance of the resurrection, his focus is on death, and there's no mention of sin at all. Death came through the type of human Adam, and now resurrection comes also through a human being, who is Christ. In the same way that we all share Adam's mortality, we share in Christ's resurrection. Again, there's nothing in these verses that argues for a sin nature. There's nothing in these verses that speaks of sin at all. Paul's intention here is to bring all of humanity into the story of God that has culminated in the resurrected Jesus. What better way to do that than to describe all of us as sharing in the experiences of Adam and then the saving grace of Christ?

The last reference we get (again from Paul) is in 2 Corinthians 11:3. This is the only allusion to Eve in all of the New Testament, and it's a fleeting one. Paul is admonishing the Corinthian church about their gullibility, their naïve willingness to listen to people who may not have their best interests in mind. He compares them to Eve, who gullibly listened to the serpent. And with good reason; it's a good metaphor for what he's trying to get them to see. But he's certainly not describing original sin, or roundly condemning Eve, or saying anything innate about a woman's nature. He's simply using Eve as an illustration. It would be similar to saying, "Don't be like your Uncle Roger who got scammed that one time." That's good advice. It isn't original sin.

A Universal Story

The rest of scripture simply doesn't seem to have the same level of obsession with Genesis 3 that Western Christianity possesses. But we can see that it is a universal story, because it touches on the human experience.

In the same way that Paul uses Adam as a type through whom we can further understand Jesus, we can see the man Adam and the woman Eve as universal types, which means we see in them something that is also true about us. We read them literarily, not literally. When we read Genesis 3, we do not have to say, "Oh yes, that's how I got to be like this. It's their fault." We can say, quite simply, "Oh yes, I am sometimes like that."

Most likely, you already read much of scripture this way. When you read a parable, or a story in the gospels, or a story of a prophet calling people to repentance, you can see yourself in the story. You can recognize the connection between your own life and the rich young ruler, or the impatient Israelites in the wilderness, or Jairus's daughter. You do not need to trace your personal ancestral history back to these individuals to feel that connection, or to understand the spiritual truth of the story. The story speaks to you, because there is a way in which you are like them. Adam and Eve, too, are characters who speak to us. We know what it means to be curious, to hide from God, to shift blame. We know. And when we read the story, we become aware of our potential to be like them. Scripture allows us to see ourselves in such a way that we can recognize our faults as well as our faith, because it is only in this self-awareness that we grow spiritually and live into the likeness of God.

As we prepare to look with fresh eyes on the story of Genesis 3, I hope we have found perspective by recognizing how the story fits into the bigger story of scripture, and have become aware of some assumptions that are keeping us stuck in unhelpful ways of reading the passage.

Let us return now to the garden, and see what we see.

God's Actions Speak Loudly of Blessing

When we read Genesis 3, we focus almost exclusively on what the story means for us—what it says about us, what we can do about it, and how we can resolve whatever problem we believe it demonstrates. What we rarely, if ever, do is ask ourselves what the story tells us about God. As people steeped in original blessing, the steadfastness of God is to be our center. Does the center hold even in the troublesome story of Genesis 3?

First, let's back up to Genesis 2. Genesis 2 is the less popular creation story. On the day God creates the heavens and the earth, no wild plants or field crops grow yet, because God has not yet sent any rain, nor anyone to till the land. Then God fashions a human out of the dust of the earth by breathing life into his nostrils. In Hebrew, there's a little play on words between the human ("adam") and the earth ("adamah"). Thanks to God's breath of life, the human of dust becomes a living being, literally an earthling.

And then God plants the garden. It's worth noting, because the text just said the reason there was not yet a garden was because there was no rain and no farmer. But God does not make the human plant the garden. God benevolently begins the work, and places the human in the garden to maintain it. The garden grows every kind of good tree with edible fruit, including the tree of life and the tree of the knowledge of good and evil. God creates woman as partner to the man, and they are naked and not ashamed.

When the man and the woman eat the fruit, we are not told how God feels about it. No verse or word gives us insight into God's emotions about it. We can only look at God's response. God walks in the garden and calls for them, an insight into the close relationship God keeps with them. When the man tells them they were hiding because they were naked, God asks, "Who told you you were naked? Have you eaten from the tree of which I commanded you not to eat?" When the man says he took the fruit from the woman, God turns to her and says, "What is this that you have done?" We do not know the tone with which God says this, but it does not say God shouted, stomped, yelled, or berated them. It does not indicate God changes temperament at all from just a moment ago when God was walking in the garden. Maybe it's anger, or disappointment. Maybe it's sadness. Maybe it's something else.

Because Genesis is a story set in contrast to other ancient Near Eastern stories, we remember the overall intent of the Genesis creation story is to present a picture not of chaos but harmony. The God of the Hebrews is not destructive or tempestuous. So though the verses do not tell us anything specific about God's tone, we can infer at the very least that

God is not a raging lunatic, or an angry tyrant, because it would go against the purpose of providing a distinctive contrast to the pagan gods of the time. God is not out of control, with a volcanically eruptive temper, unlike Marduk and Tiamat of the *Enuma Elish*, or other Babylonian stories. God is even-tempered, in control, responsive and not reactive.

Blessings and Curses

When the man lays the blame on the woman, and the woman lays blame on the serpent, God responds in backwards order, first to the serpent, then the woman, then the man. Though this next section does contain two curses, neither are directed at the woman or the man. God does not remove original blessing, and God does not bestow a curse, either.

First, God tells the serpent it is cursed among all the animals. The symbol of the serpent is rich and complex, which we will discuss in more detail later. But for now, as we consider this story in its ancient Near Eastern context, it's worth pointing out that the serpent was seen in many pagan religions as a god, or at least as a symbol of a god or goddess. Sometimes the serpent was a symbol of chaos itself. For God to stand over against the serpent as its creator is a declaration of God's sovereignty. Again, the Hebrew God is the source of all life. And when God curses the serpent and declares it will crawl on its belly for the rest of its days, it's a definitive declaration of who serves whom. Some interpreters believe this is the heart of the story, a call to God's people to beware of the gods of the Canaanite religion, and for all future readers, to beware of any other adversary that moves us away from life with God.

Second, God tells the man the ground will be cursed because of him. For us to understand this curse, we need to remember the wider context of Genesis 2, where the man is placed in the garden to till and tend the soil. God plants the garden, and sends rain upon it, and as God's creation, the soil is designed to bring life. Basically, the man has a pretty easy job. Life is going to flourish with minimal effort on his part. After they eat of the fruit, God curses the ground (not the man), and tells the man his farming vocation will now be much more difficult, including sweat, thorns, and thistles.

While this shift is hardly a good one, it is not a comprehensive one. Despite the curse, the ground still does exactly what it is designed to do. It brings life, just as it was intended, albeit with more effort. Life will not come as easily, but it will still flourish with effort. God doesn't say, "I am plucking up this whole garden and making you start over, and forget about the rain because I'm not sending it." God doesn't say, "The ground is cursed and you won't be able to grow so much as a turnip anymore." And God definitely doesn't say, "This land is worthless now! Forget that I ever called it good!" Farming the land goes from easy to difficult. But the integrity of the land and the call of the farmer remain the same.

We can say the same for the consequences (not curses) God describes to the man and the woman. Childbirth will be harder, relationships will be harder, tilling the soil will be harder. And this difficulty will last to the end of our human days. But God does not say anything about removing blessing. God does not say, "Well, you're no good any longer. I take it back." God doesn't say, "You now will have difficulty having a relationship with me because you have a sin nature that will block you from it." God doesn't say, "Now sin will be passed on through you to all generations, and thanks to you, death is going to happen." It's just nonsensical to read so much into the text like that, especially when so much is at stake.

After God issues these two curses to the snake and the ground, God makes garments for the man and the woman, and clothes them. And the clothes God provides are a vast improvement over the fig leaves the man and woman made themselves; they are leather garments, which will be soft and keep them warm and stand up to the weather. God sees their vulnerability and covers them. God does not tell them to get over their nakedness and deal with it. God doesn't force them to stand out in the cold, buck naked, for punishment. God simply covers them. Whatever consequences exist because of their actions, God's kindness remains. God's blessing is ever abundant. They still belong to God, and God still cares for them.

The early church father Irenaeus said the man and the woman made themselves clothes out of fig leaves because fig leaves are itchy and uncomfortable, and they felt they deserved nothing better.[1] In response, God replaces their

1. Irenaeus, *Against Heresies*, 3.23.5.

clothing of harsh leaves with supple leather garments instead. Though we don't know why the man and woman used fig leaves, I know so many heartbreaking stories of people who feel trapped in their own sense of guilt and punish and judge themselves so harshly. Sometimes it's hard enough to believe and accept that God wants to clothe us anyway, much less provide us with clothes far better than we had before.

I am reminded of Isaiah 61, a passage that reflects many of the themes of the garden. Isaiah brings good news to the oppressed and brokenhearted of a God who gives a garland instead of ashes, the oil of gladness instead of mourning, the mantle of praise instead of a faint spirit. God returns blessing for our shame, and clothes us with the gifts of God's goodness. We see God respond to us with loving-kindness over and over again in the pages of scripture.

God's actions remind me of a word of praise in Jewish tradition, *dayenu*. Dayenu means "it would have been enough." As a form of prayer and praise, someone says, "It would have been enough, Lord, if you had given me this one thing. But you have given me so much more!" It's a way of seeing God's abundance in our own lives, of practicing gratitude. Just breath itself would have been enough, but God gives us friendship and love, comfort and kindness. What abundance! The fig leaves would have been enough, but God upgraded their fig leaves to leather garments. Instead of seeing Genesis 3 as a story of fallenness, perhaps we can see that moment in the garden as the first moment in scripture that humanity experienced dayenu.

The Tree of Life

After God clothes the man and the woman, we get to eavesdrop on God's inner dialogue. Now that they know the difference between good and evil, God does not want the man and the woman to eat of the tree of life and live forever. God sends them out of the garden not to banish them for eating the fruit, but to prevent them from eating from the tree of life. God even stations winged creatures and a flaming sword to guard the way to the tree of life.

What is that all about?

Early church father John Chrysostom considered this to be the most gracious thing God could do.[2] It was not yet time for the man and the woman to live forever. These two trees provided a way for them to practice obedience and disobedience. If they stayed in the garden and ate from the tree of life, they would be stuck in disobedience forever. It would have been arrested development, a story unfinished.

It's interesting to note that God never prohibited them from eating from the tree of life, so they presumably could have eaten it at any time. God isn't apparently concerned with humans living forever, unless it will freeze them in a state of being (or, more accurately, becoming) that's less than God intended.

Leaving the Garden

The man and the woman's relationship with God changes after they eat the fruit, but when we look closely this change

2. Chrysostom, John. "Homily 18." *Homilies on Genesis.*

is far less violent than it's often been painted. It's certainly not a declaration that all humanity is inherently bent toward evil from now on. This change has two components. First, they hide from God because they now know they are naked. God responds by providing them clothing. Second, they leave Eden and a cherubim and sword now guard the entrance to Eden. God does this not as punishment, but for their own protection. So the last question is, *how* did God send the man and the woman away to leave the garden?

The Hebrew verb that describes their leaving, *weysalehehu*, has been translated as "banished," "sent away," "expelled," "sent out," and "sent forth." As with many Hebrew words, the definitions vary greatly and depend greatly on context. The Bible I used most frequently growing up was the NIV, which uses the word "banished." But most modern scholars have agreed this is not the appropriate translation, and now many say "sent out" or "sent forth" instead. So which is it: Were they banished, or sent forth? This particular word is used three other times in scripture. Let's take a look at those stories and see how it can help us with context.

The first story in 2 Samuel 3 is a convoluted story of intrigue, ending in the duplicitous murder of Abner, the general of Saul's armies. A good deal of bad blood exists between Israel and Judah, and particularly between Abner and Joab, King David's general and nephew. But *weysalehehu* is used a number of times to describe Abner's interactions with David, the King of Judah, which by comparison are straightforward and positive. Abner comes to David to give him reports from different regions, and David is pleased with what he hears. Then Abner asks David if he can go to assemble the people for David, and David sends him to do this. Joab arrives and asks David, "Where's Abner?" And David says he sent him away in peace. Joab is angry, because David shows favor to Abner, who Joab considers an enemy. So it's very clear in this story that *weysalehehu* is not just a sending, but a sending in peace.

Secondly, in 1 Kings 20, Ben-hadad, King of Aram, is in a military tug-of-war with the king of Israel. When Ben-hadad finally surrenders, he sends word to the king and asks for mercy, promising to return the lands he has taken by force. They make a treaty, and the king then sends him away in peace. Even though there has been ill will between them, they are reconciled and Ben-hadad is sent away in peace.

Lastly, in Jeremiah 40:5, the prophet Jeremiah learns that he is being released from prison in Ramah. The captain of the guard tells Jeremiah he can either come with them to Babylon under their care, or go wherever else he wants. Jeremiah decides to go elsewhere, and they send him off with provisions for his journey.

In all three of these instances, *weysalehehu* is the act of being sent off in peace. And there's no reason for us to think that what happened in Genesis is any different.

God chooses to prevent the man and the woman from eating from the tree of life. That means they do have to leave the garden. This is not a punishment but a protective measure. God sends them out not in wrath or in anger, but in peace. They are not able to return to the garden, but this is not some sort of divine spanking. In fact, we may find that it is rather a divine sending forth.

A New Season

When the man and the woman choose to eat the fruit and are sent out, they are portrayed not as humans who are at the unpredictable and violent whims of their gods, but humans who are given freedom and provision, even after they choose poorly. Again we see a contrast between ancient Near Eastern stories of chaos that began with evil gods and resulted in evil throughout creation, and how Genesis boldly declares a creation marked by goodness and harmony. If there is chaos, the biblical story tells us it comes from human choice, not from a vengeful or bombastic God.

Rather than seeing humans as passive recipients of the gods' bad moods, humans have agency to move toward God in harmony, or away from God toward chaos. This isn't only a revolutionary view of God, but a revolutionary view of humans, too. It's the one-two punch of original blessing we will see over and over again throughout the biblical story: God has created us good and blessed us, and we have been given the agency to choose our path in life, which will either keep us near that goodness or move us away from it. Our goodness is both an origin and a goal, but the blessing we have been given by God remains constant. From beginning to end, God desires for us to keep near this harmony, this goodness, no matter the cost, and no matter our choices.

Even when we move away from God, God moves toward us, seeking to close the distance.

Genesis 3 is a story of blessing and curses, because we live in a world of both. But as people of faith, we also know that curses will not have the last word.

You Can't Rush Happily Ever After

I generally dislike "what if" questions because they have a tendency to keep us focused on the past and stuck in coulds/shoulds/woulds rather than propelling us to move forward. But as we look to Genesis 3 with fresh eyes, I think a "what if" question provides us with a good deal of perspective. What if the man and the woman never ate from the tree of good and evil?

Well, there wouldn't be anything to read after Genesis 3. The man and the woman would go on living happily in the harmony of the garden and maybe have a family. And if none of the children ever ate from the tree, then they would live happily and maybe have a family and it would go on and on and on. They would all live happily ever after, forever and ever.

Which is boring, for one thing. The only reason happily ever after is a satisfying ending is because it comes only after things are not happy and not at all settled. Nobody would ever read Genesis 1–3 if that's all there was, because it would not only be boring, but completely unhelpful to our lives.

Have you ever read a story where the whole plot was nothing but smooth sailing? Of course you haven't. They aren't stories worth telling.

The stories we're most drawn to reading, the epic stories, all contain what Joseph Campbell calls the hero's journey. Everything is going along as usual, and then the main character is invited into an adventure. The adventure will bring certain disruption, and even danger, but as the character confronts different obstacles in search of something precious, we see her emerge at the end as a hero. She has come to know something true and important about herself and the world, and she has grown capable of far greater things because of it.

Many compelling heroes in literature bring us along on this journey: Harry Potter, Bilbo and Frodo Baggins, the Pevensie children in Narnia, Tom Sawyer, Dorothy in Oz, King Arthur, Meg Murray, Luke Skywalker, Katniss Everdeen, just to name a few. And it's worth noting that when a character doesn't stay on the path until the redemptive end, they become villains. Something destructive happens, which is how we end up with evil queens and corrupt empires and terrifying witches/wizards and Darth Vader. It's just one more example of why original sin doesn't actually make common sense to us. When a person turns toward evil, we don't call it destiny. We call it tragedy.

So when we come to the garden, which is the womb in which the story of God is birthed, perhaps the best question we can ask is, "What can this tell us about who we are to become?"

For us to understand that, we actually have to begin by talking about that pesky serpent.

One Sneaky Snake

A Jewish rabbinical commentary on Genesis 3 describes the serpent as "a creature of enduring mystery."[1] That is the simplest and clearest description one could hope for. Many people have such tightly held assumptions about snakes. Aren't snakes evil and terrible and life-threatening? Is there anything more to it than that?! The answer is a resounding, reverberating yes. There is far, far more.

My dear friend Luke is just terrified of snakes. He is not terrified of most anything else, but the mere mention of a snake causes him to visibly shudder. I find his fear a little bit funny and maybe even slightly entertaining, so I was pestering him about it one day. "What is it about snakes that you hate so much?!" I asked bemused. (He did not share the sentiment.) "Danielle, have you SEEN snakes? They don't have legs. How do they even move like that?!" But of course, this is precisely why snakes are so richly symbolic. They are a mystery to us. We don't even know how they move like that!

In a literary sense, we should be far more surprised if a serpent had not made an appearance in the early stories of Genesis. To say that serpents were ubiquitous in the ancient world is perhaps an understatement. Serpents figured prominently not only in stories, but in carvings, jewelry,

1. David L. Lieber and Jules Harlow, *Etz Hayim: Torah and Commentary* (Philadelphia: Jewish Publication Society, 2001), 17.

pottery, stories, and architecture. Even so, the meaning of the serpent in all of these varied contexts is nothing near one-dimensional. It is as if each attempt to capture what the snake symbolized somehow kept falling short, and so the project was started over and over again. Or, conversely, the snake obviously meant a good number of recognizable things to the majority of people in the ancient Near East, so the vast usage of symbolism was not confusing but expected.

And what was this symbolism? What made the snake so prominent and central? One of my seminary professors, James Charlesworth, studied serpent symbolism in the ancient world for a decade and enumerated thirty-two distinct reasons.[2] Thirty-two! Can you imagine?! A snake sheds its skin, so it is a symbol of rebirth. Because it can move quietly and often without detection, it is cunning. Snakes carry venom and so they symbolize death and danger; conversely, they kill animals harmful to humans, so they are also called guardians. Since snakes till the ground and kill mice and rodents, they have been used as a sign of fruitfulness, of fertile soil. This is what led some rabbis to remark that every Jewish garden should have a snake, much like today we place worms in our compost bin. That's not all thirty-two reasons, but it's a start.

Anyone who has studied medicine is familiar with the Rod of Asclepius, the symbol of a staff encircled by a serpent. It is commonly confused with the caduceus, the symbol of two snakes intertwined on a central staff. Though both are now

2. James H. Charlesworth, *The Good and Evil Serpent: How a Universal Symbol Became Christianized* (New Haven: Yale University Press, 2010).

emblems of medicine and healing, the Rod of Asclepius is technically the original emblem. Asclepius was the god of healing in Greek mythology. (If you remember the story from the gospels of the lame man being healed in the pools of Bethesda, it takes place at one of the many temples to Asclepius where people gathered for healing.) So the image of Asclepius' rod, encircled with a snake, communicated powerful healing. The serpent has long been used in conjunction with medicine because physicians realize that they hold the power of both life and death in their hands. When a physician takes the Hippocratic oath, she vows to use her knowledge to bring healing and life, and not poison or death. It is a necessary vow.

My friend Dana is a nurse anesthetist, which means she spends every day putting just the right amount of medicine in people's bloodstreams to sedate them, but not enough to kill them. She said the snake is an appropriate symbol of medicine because all medicine is actually poison. It's how much and when you use the poison that makes it healing or deadly. The right amount of medicine will alleviate a woman's labor pains, while too much would stop her heart. It is an incredibly precarious balance. This reminded me of a book I read repeatedly as a child, about Louis Pasteur and his breakthrough on vaccines. Many of his contemporaries thought he was insane to believe that putting a small bit of a virus into the body could ever lead to the body's immunity against the virus. But, of course, they were wrong, and Pasteur's breakthrough has saved literally millions of lives since. The ancients knew this deep wisdom long before modern science could explain it. Sometimes a little poison is necessary to be healed.

There is an ancient primeval quality to snakes, clearly evident long before we knew they had outlived the dinosaurs. Because snakes swallow their prey whole (I can hear Luke shuddering now), they convey a sense of totality. There is nothing piecemeal about snakes. We take them entirely, or not at all, in the same way they take their prey. And similarly, it often takes us quite a long time to digest the symbolism. Because the head and the tail of the snake look similarly, some symbols depict a serpent with heads on both ends, while others depict the snake in a circle, with the head biting its tail. This emphasis on completeness, on totality, has been pondered by alchemists and poets and storytellers for generations. So it may be common for us to say we can't make heads or tails of it, but when it comes to snake imagery, that means we've arrived at wholeness.

When I first read about this head-to-tail serpentine symbol, which is called the ourobouros, I thought immediately of *The Neverending Story*, whose amulet shows this very thing. (Do you remember that big brown book with the two golden snakes entwined in a figure-eight symbol of infinity, biting each other's tails?) If you know that story at all, you will perhaps understand more aptly all the serpent entails: danger, risk, adventure, even loss, but also growth, completeness, and an eternal quality. Bastian, the protagonist, begins the book as an uncertain, self-doubting boy and emerges by the end as a young man who has learned he is capable of great love, and is brave enough to express it. (Yet another hero's journey.)

To return to the words of the rabbinical commentary, the serpent is a creature of enduring mystery. In Genesis 3, I believe the serpent represents that which it declares—good and evil, and all the knowledge of both. In fact, this overarching sense of complex oneness is at the heart of serpent symbolism. It is head and tail, poison and medicine. Serpents are a primitive and sacred *both/and*.

The Garden Snake

In Genesis 3, the serpent is clearly part of God's created order. Though that may make you feel unsettled, it actually ought to do the opposite. The biblical story of creation, remember, is a story of order and harmony. The serpent is not independent of God, but part of God's creation. This would have been a noticeable distinction from the role of the serpent in pagan religions of the time, where the serpent was an emblem of the god or goddess, and therefore an equal. The Genesis story clearly implies there is no life outside of God, even for a symbol of immortality. In the Hebrew scriptures, this will always be the refrain as the Hebrew people sought to distinguish themselves from their pagan counterparts. All come from God, and all must respond to God.

Because the serpent is part of God's created order, we have to consider it a normal and natural part of the garden, too. Whatever the serpent is, he is not foreign. The text does not say the serpent snuck into the garden unbidden. God does not react to the serpent as if it is trespassing. There is no creation outside of what God has made, and so the serpent arrives on the scene unknown and yet assumed.

As we read the story literarily, we recognize the serpent as a narrative device. The serpent presents a turning point, or what is commonly called the inciting incident. In a story, everything before the inciting incident is backstory. Backstory is given in the first section of pages in a novel, or the first few minutes of a movie. It sets up the world of the story for you. The inciting incident then introduces a turning point, conflict, or crisis, so that the real story may begin. The serpent is the inciting incident, because we wouldn't have a story without the events of Genesis 3. The story simply must move beyond the garden.

Serpents have been used often as central characters in inciting incidents. Because a serpent can be at the same time poisonous and necessary for healing, they often convey the kind of turning point that sends our protagonists on to their destinies. In this way, the serpent is both good and bad. It brings trouble, or at least presents it, like in our Genesis 3 story. But it also provides the necessary conflict that will send humanity toward eternal life. The symbol of the serpent makes a full circle, and returns to being an emblem of immortality. Though it will not come in the garden, or without turmoil, the woman and the man now move toward eternal life in a new and broader way.

To put it another way, Genesis 3 is an ending that makes way for a new beginning. The backstory of creation now moves toward the plot development of human history. This beginning will quickly come to yet another symbolic narrative ending—the flood—only to find itself at the beginning once again. This pattern will repeat thematically throughout the pages of scripture, until we find ourselves in yet another garden at the end of the gospels, where the new beginning of Easter awaits us. And then, finally, scripture leaves us with the imagery in Revelation, where God will once again walk among us face to face, amid trees whose leaves bring healing to all the nations. But God will walk among us not in the confines of the garden, but in the great expanse of the city. Even God doesn't stay in Eden forever.

Three Alternative Readings

We can learn a lot from the ways our Jewish brothers and sisters read the scriptures. They didn't cave to a Western rationalism that requires every story to have one interpretation, or one moral, or one way of reading. Which, if you think about it, is a preposterous thing to ask of holy scriptures, or of God. The kind of truth we engage is far bigger than that, and we do nothing but harm the text when we seek to limit or control it. So let's begin by acknowledging there are a good number of legitimate ways to interpret Genesis 3. I happen to think the most popular Protestant version of it is one of the least legitimate ones, if only because of the unconvincing conclusions it makes about original sin. So I'd like to share what I consider to be three more viable options, none of which require you to belittle your relationship with God or your own dignity to believe them.

1: No Other Gods before Me

The first reading is quite simple, and I've already mentioned it before. Genesis 3 can be interpreted as a warning story against false gods. If we see the serpent as a symbol of pagan religion, then the serpent's role in the story is to make the man and woman question and turn away from God. For the first hearers of these stories, faithfulness to the Hebrew God in a culture of many competing gods was a defining struggle. Most scholars believe Genesis was written when the Israelites were in exile during the Babylonian empire, spread out across a number of foreign nations. Much of the Old Testament bears witness to their struggle.

If we see Genesis 3 as a story warning us to stay faithful to God, we also see it as a sign of God's faithfulness to us. God is the unquestionable Creator, who holds even the pagan gods of other religions to account. And God is the gracious provider, even after the man and woman have turned away. We can read the story with this basic understanding and have all that we need, without any damaging excess baggage.

If we want to add another layer of complexity to this reading, we can recognize that the serpent encourages the man and woman to disobey God, and pushes them toward knowledge instead. Knowing good and evil is not inherently bad, but when it is separated from relationship with God, it becomes problematic. The tree of the knowledge of good and evil is meant to stand beside the tree of life. God has planted the garden like that for a reason. Knowledge and wisdom must be together, or else we lose our way.

If we look at Psalm 1, we see echoes of this very theme. The happy person doesn't follow wicked advice (hear that, serpent?) but loves the Lord's instruction. This person is like a tree planted by streams of water (sound familiar?) which bears fruit at just the right time. But the wicked are like dust (heard that before?) and won't stand with the just or the righteous. We see this theme over and over again in the wisdom literature of Psalms, Proverbs, Ecclesiastes, and more. The righteous are those who follow the wise ways of God.

Most of the terrifying figures in history have been intellectually smart. They knew how to use knowledge as a weapon for their own devices. And we will see this same pattern play out very soon in the book of Genesis itself, when God looks upon the people in the city of Babel who decide to build a tower up to the heavens. Knowledge is power, but outside of God, knowledge is destructive power and not life-giving power. With knowledge we have pioneered life-extending surgeries and atomic bombs. With knowledge we have streamlined farming and decimated forests. With knowledge we have built communities of belonging and reigns of terror. So knowledge is not inherently bad, but knowledge by itself cannot save us. Knowledge, separated from wisdom, is its own false god.

2: Prodigal Children

We can see the garden as a universal description of our relationship with God. There are times when we walk closely with God, and there are times when we question and disobey.

When we misstep, God remains committed to us, but we also live in a connected world where consequences are a natural response to movement away from God. As we recognize the realities of life away from God, we are encouraged to move toward God once again, trusting that transformation and new life await us.

If we want to see this story through the lens of a well-known parable, we could compare Genesis 3 to the story of the prodigal son. The prodigal son thought he could make his own way outside of his family, and so he set off alone, only to return when he realized there was nothing but struggle waiting for him in a world without a relationship with his father. So it was with the prodigal son, and so it was with the man and the woman, and so it is with us. Scripture invites us to consider whether we have left home, all the while reminding us that it is God who calls us back to life, and God who makes a way for us to return, and God who welcomes us upon arrival.

Genesis 3 is the first story that reveals the point and counterpoint of sin and grace, but it's a story that will keep repeating. I heard renowned Old Testament scholar Walter Brueggemann describe all of scripture by saying, "There are only betrayals and reconciliations."[3] How true. Over and over again, we falter only to find the God who redeems us and calls us home.

3. Walter Brueggemann, Perkins School of Theology Ministers Week, February 1, 2016.

3. Growing Up

Though I find resonance with both of the ways of reading the story above, I'm most partial to the one I saved for last, because I believe it best holds both the beauty and complexity of the story, and of our story. And that is to see Genesis 3 as a coming-of-age story.

We remember in Genesis 2 that the world is described as a fertile field, and within that field there is a garden. God has done most of the work in the garden, so the man and the woman have a few chores, but they have it pretty easy. They are safe, protected from the wider world to a degree. They have everything they could need, including animals and room to explore and companionship and someone to love and watch over them. What does that sound like? Eden sounds to me like a happy childhood. And though it's not one everyone experiences in their own lives, if we want to understand our place in the family of God, we can see what it is like to be a child of our Creator, where we are indeed loved unconditionally. If the garden is an idealistic version of anything, it's the ideal childhood home.

The man and the woman were raised in the garden, but eventually they would have to leave home. And, like every other child who embarks toward adulthood, leaving home inevitably includes some form of individuation and rebellion. For us to become ourselves, we have to push against the very people who made us. We have to stand against them, and even reject them, in order to find our way back into relationship with them again as adults. This is the reality of human experience.

The man and the woman grew up, because that's the natural thing to do. And when you grow up, you start to want to assert your independence, and sometimes you question your parents regardless of how well meaning they are. You want to make your own choices. You want to choose your own path. You want to do something forbidden, even, just to see what happens. This is not the end of the world. This is the beginning of adulthood. It's natural, and necessary, and maybe it's why God put that tree in the garden to begin with. What happens after they eat the fruit? Their eyes are opened, which sounds like a good metaphor for growing up. They realize they are naked, which has nothing to do with sex or even with shame but is just an acknowledgment that they are now realizing they are embodied people in a different way than they understood before.

If we see the man and the woman as children (who become teenagers), the story makes much more sense. We can imagine children frolicking around the garden without giving much thought to the one tree they're told not to touch. And when we look at the woman's response to the serpent, when she says God told them not to eat it, or even touch it, we can think of so many examples of children who naturally exaggerate the rules of their parents to make a point. They aren't adult robots who one day got duped by a shrewd serpent. They are curious children, who eventually came to find the question of rebellion appealing as teenagers. In fact, some Jewish commentators have described the serpent as a spirit of rebellion that arises in adolescence. Some parents of teenagers can likely understand what they mean.

We can understand why they are naked and unashamed, too. Children only become aware of their nakedness when they become old enough to recognize their distinction from the opposite sex. That's not a bad thing, or even a shameful thing. It's an age-appropriate thing. I remember when my daughter started closing the door to her bathroom, and walking into my son's room one day only to have him utter a mortified shriek that he was changing clothes. From one day to the next, I had to respect their new boundaries for modesty. It's simply a natural part of growing up. Adam and Eve bear children after they leave the garden not because sex is bad but because you have to travel through puberty first.

Second-century theologian Irenaeus believed the man and the woman are children in the garden, too, and this view of the story was a common view of the early church. Once naked and unashamed, they embark upon adulthood the moment they gain knowledge of good and evil. What is broken in the garden was obedience, not original blessing. What is broken was not the image of God but the innocence of children. And yet, we cannot hold onto this innocence forever. We have to learn to find the qualities of innocence in our growing capacity to see God in the midst of a troubled and troubling world. The man and the woman carry with them not the stoic essence of perfection, but the image of God, as well as the potential to grow into the likeness of God.

And they have to find their way into a new, more mature relationship with God, one chosen on their own terms.

In the practices of the church, we respect and honor this process in the way we move children toward adult faith. In traditions that baptize infants, the church offers confirmation, where students are invited to ask questions and to redefine their faith not as one their parents gave them but as one they choose for themselves. In other traditions, baptism itself is the way a person claims the story as her own, and chooses to walk in the ways of Jesus. For our Jewish brothers and sisters, bar and bat mitzvahs invite teens literally to become children of the commandments. For though faith is in great part inherited, it must always also be chosen, if it is to be genuine at all. When we think of faith, we could say that God does not want an arranged covenant with us. God wants us to choose to love God freely, on our own terms.

Humanity cannot love God for God's own sake if there is never any option to love differently. And so each of us must find our way to God only by honestly reviewing all our options. That's the way it works. Faithfulness is a choice. God chooses over and over again to be faithful to us, and God has freely given us the choice of whether to be faithful to God. So though we are born in the love of God, and we remain in the blessing of God no matter where we go, we make our way to God in a world of competing loyalties. And we must decide where our hearts will find their home.

Medieval Christian mystic Hildegard of Bingen believed we are all born with original wisdom, and it comes to us as children like a tent folded up. As we grow, our task is to set up the tent, to begin to live in it, to find shelter and spaciousness and comfort within it. The wisdom we receive is present at birth, but it also expands as we grow and find our home within wisdom's tent.

Life in the garden is a lovely childhood. As in all loving homes, the man and the woman have everything they need: a loving parent, their basic needs provided, a little bit of work to give them structure but not enough to give them hassle, and the joy and wonderment of innocence. But as every parent knows, you cannot shield your children from the realities of life forever. Snakes exist, and evil exists, and questions will undoubtedly arise. Why can't I do that? Who says you know best? What happens if I do this? At some point, our innocent eyes are opened. We see the world for what it really is, a perplexing knot of good and evil, blessing and curse, God and not-God.

The man and the woman stumble into this knowledge, which is usually how it goes with us, too. Sometimes we brazenly choose rebellion, but more often, we make a choice that seems innocuous enough until we realize afterward we've changed something profound. Many parents of teenagers will tell you how they asked their teen, "Didn't you think that through?" only to be answered with blank stares. No. Of course they didn't. They are just learning to understand what's at stake, the same way we did.

When their eyes are opened, they see the reality of the world, plain as day: the world is full of choices, and when you make them, you will forever be caught between stabilizing and destabilizing forces. In fact, the act of being human is itself both stabilizing and destabilizing. Welcome to the real world.

Every parent has a moment when she recognizes her child realizes he has options. He doesn't have to do what you say. He can choose differently. Your whole parenting game has to change at that point. You can no longer assume your child will follow your rules. You have to find more appropriate boundaries, but by default, now they are bigger ones. Though it's always a bit disconcerting at first, consider the alternative; if your child never learns this, he will never grow up. At some point, innocence becomes infantilism. We do have one story about that—it's Peter Pan. Peter never wants to leave Neverland, but Wendy wisely realizes it is better to grow up. And it is, even if the process is always bittersweet.

In our modern society, helicopter parents are those who shield their children from the tension of the knowledge of good and evil. They do not want their children to feel the strain between the two polarizing forces, so they remove conflict, smooth over difficulties, cushion falls. They remove all obstacles, take consequences out of all choices. They want their children to be safe, but in the process, they prevent their children from learning to become wise.

God is decidedly not a helicopter parent. God places the tree and the snake in the garden because they are necessary. If we are to live into the image of God, we cannot remain infants, or children, or even teenagers. We must become disciples, who fashion our lives of faith by making choices, day after day after day.

In our culture, we so prize youth that we circulate stories

still about the fountain of youth, which we act out in plastic surgeries and fad diets and clothing choices and all kinds of things. We are living in a society that so overvalues youthfulness that we never are asked to grow up. True success is to be young forever. What a powerful counternarrative Genesis 3 offers us, which says, actually, God's not that obsessed with your youth. God wants you to keep growing and becoming. What a powerful course corrective for a society that is more and more infantilized.

Growing up is anything but easy. We can feel so foolish when we realize the world has been this complex all along. We feel naked and vulnerable in the face of such an overwhelming onslaught of conflicting information. Carlos Mesters wrote, "To become aware of evil is a shattering experience."[4] I would add, becoming aware we are capable of evil is an equally shattering one. As teenagers, we unfortunately learn the realities of both.

But we remember that God creates all the world good, which includes both the safe protection of the garden and the expansive complexity of the fertile land. Indeed, God fashions the man from the fertile land itself, and only afterward places him in the safe confines of the garden. After they eat the fruit, God sends the man and the woman back into the fertile land, to find their way and farm the soil, and, eventually, to discover God's goodness even among the thistles and thorns.

We were never meant to live only in the garden. God creates the fertile land as the intended territory of human

---

4. Carlos Mesters, *Eden, Golden Age or Goad to Action?* (Maryknoll, NY: Orbis, 1974), 52.

experience. What we need to know most of all as we embark, though, is that we come from a place of safe loving-care, with a Divine Parent who loves us and is faithful to us, a God to whom we can always come home. The story of Genesis 3 is our story: we begin with God, we go out with God, only so that we can again find our home in God.

The Curse of Knowledge

Though we've already talked about the curse God brings upon the serpent and upon the land, we can now see the other admonitions within a more proper context. God speaks both to the man and the woman, and God's responses differ based on their role as giver-of-life and cultivator-of-life. Even as I type that, I shudder to imagine anyone taking that too literally. (One of my college professors encouraged us to hold our theological beliefs like a porcupine. Squeeze them too tight and you bleed. It's the same for our readings of scripture. Squeeze them too literally and they cut us.) In this story, and not as a declaration of manhood and womanhood always and everywhere, the man and woman are known by their role as the farmer of the land and the mother of all living things. We can see these in light of the overarching story of Creator God as one who brings life, and as God's image-bearers, we too are called to bring forth life.

For the woman Eve, who will be named the mother of all the living, this will come most clearly through childbirth. She will not create as God creates, with the ease of a word. She is not God, and she creates life out of the tangled fabric of life on earth. Genesis 3:16, usually translated, "Your desire will be for your husband," has been so commonly used as a justification for patriarchy, but the scope of the word here is far more specific. She will long for her husband, because only with him can she be the bearer of life. But that desire, that urge, is now set in a world of both good and evil, where it may also do her great harm. The word used here is the same used in Song of Songs, though; so the desire itself is not inherently bad, only complicated. It is a knowledge both good and evil. I actually think of the many women throughout the Old Testament—Sarah, for one—whose longing for a child proves to be conflicting. The woman Eve is called to bear life, not demand it.

For the man Adam, his work in farming the land, which came so easily for him in the garden, will now require sweat and tears, if not blood. As often in the poetic nature of Hebrew, the same word is used for the toil of the woman in childbearing and the toil of the man in farming. As I mentioned before, the good earth is still just that; it will produce life just as God designed it. But now it will require far more than a child's helping hand to tend it. For the man, the irony is that the ground from which he was fashioned is now the source of his struggle. He is but dust, and he is a living being on God's terms alone. And yet, we remember that God's terms are blessing and steadfast love. But the man Adam is called to tend life, not demand it.

A Jewish commentary suggested that the knowledge of good and evil may be more aptly described as the realization of mortality. As children, we don't yet understand that we (or anyone else) are capable of dying. When we do, we must come to terms with the fragility of life, and the fear of death.

Childbirth and farming are both tasks that connect us to life, but they also bring us face-to-face with the tension of death and the threat of the failure of life. This tension is at the heart of knowing both good and evil. We know now what harmony costs, and how difficult it is to maintain. Though animals gather food and mate with little thought, human life is both more difficult and more rewarding.

The truth is, suffering is part of life. And when we're children, we are shielded from it if we're lucky, but there comes a time when we realize that life often comes at a cost. God tells the man life from the soil will come at a cost. There will be sweat on his brow. God tells the woman life from her body will come at a cost. There will be pain in childbirth. This is the natural result of knowing good and evil. And it's the natural result of living in the tension of life and death, blessing and curse. Our growth and maturity comes from within that tension. It comes from nowhere else.

Bearing life and bringing life is not always easy. It is natural, but it is not without effort. As we get older, we come to understand that life is both precious and costly, both gift and charge. At the intersection of these tensions, we find our vocation, our holy calling. We are to be God's image-bearers even in the midst of life's difficulties.

Children of God

When we see Genesis 3 as a coming-of-age story, we can

affirm what we most need to know about ourselves, which is that we are children of God who often pull away from God, and to great consequence. Our life is in God and with God, and when we disconnect from God, we only find disharmony and degradation. Our life with God is in fact so central that it affects our relationship with everything else, too, with other people and with the earth itself. To walk in conflict with God is to seek our own ruin and in fact the ruin of our world. We cannot become wise adults if we do not face the gravity of our responsibility to choose well.

But we also find we can approach ourselves, and others, with a deep well of grace. All of this stumbling and blundering about is just part of the process of growing up. As much as we wish it weren't so, there's really no way around it. Nobody wants to go through the awkward stages of middle school or the self-doubt of teenage years, but nobody gets a pass. The only way out is through, so we face our failings for what they are: one more step along the journey we are making toward God. And we may find when we accept it, we can find wisdom on the other side of even our worst decisions.

We are not evil villains but wayward children. We do not have a sin nature but a human nature, which includes both intimacy and isolation, communion and rebellion. We come to realize God has mercy on us because we are not yet finished, and there is hope for us yet. We come to recognize that love has always and will always cover a multitude of sins. We come to trust that neither height nor depth can separate us from the love of Christ, who is for us and with us even when we are most vehemently against ourselves. We are not left naked and ashamed, but clothed in God's righteousness, because God has upgraded even our traveling clothes.

So we learn in the garden that we are capable of good and evil, and that we often do not know the difference. But more importantly, we learn in the garden that we are loved, that we are clothed and sent away in peace, and that God is waiting for us even east of Eden.

III. Rethinking Sin

East of Eden

If we are looking for a biblical view of sin, the best place to start is in Genesis 4, not Genesis 3. Genesis 4:7 marks the first time the word "sin" is used in scripture. When God looks favorably on the offering Abel brings and doesn't look favorably on the offering Cain brings, Cain becomes angry and resentful. And God says to him, "Why are you angry, and why has your countenance fallen? If you do well, will you not be accepted? And if you do not do well, sin is lurking at the door; its desire is for you, but you must master it."[1]

Cain does not master it. He kills his brother Abel, and he is cursed by God. It's a harrowing story of jealousy, violence, and alienation. But at its heart, it is a story about blessing.

Cain and Abel both work with the land, Cain as a farmer and Abel as a shepherd. Both bring offerings to God. I have no more idea than you do why God looks favorably upon Abel's offering and not on Cain's. I don't think we need to draw any universal conclusions about it. Like the serpent, the offerings are an inciting incident, and the point of the story is what happens next. And what happens is that Cain resents

1. Genesis 4:6–7.

it. He resents it so much he takes Abel out into the fields, out into the very fertile land God has created for them and has given them, and he kills him.

Just like in the garden, God comes quickly to the scene. But unlike in the garden, God doesn't ask, "Where are you?" but instead "Where is your brother Abel?" And unlike in the garden, when the man answers honestly, "We were hiding because we were naked," Cain flat out lies. "I don't know," he says. "What am I, my brother's keeper?"

When the man answers God in the garden, God wants to find out who told them they were naked. But God does not need to find out anything with Cain. Abel's blood is crying out to God from the ground. So God doesn't say, "Who told you you weren't your brother's keeper?" Because, of course, he is. God says instead, "What have you done?"

God does not wait for Cain's reply. Instead, God tells Cain he is cursed from the very ground that received his brother's blood, and this time, God does say there will be no life in it for him any longer. Murder is deep rebellion against the God of Life, and it does not go unpunished.

Cain is overwhelmed by the consequences of his actions. He tells God, "My punishment is more than I can bear. Today you have driven me away from the soil, and I shall be hidden from your face; I shall be a fugitive and a wanderer on the earth, and anyone who meets me may kill me." Cain recognizes the two primary gifts he has been given: the fertile land God created, and the presence of God. So he's understandably dismayed when it seems he will be stripped of both. What else can that mean but certain death?

But God does not respond with death, because God is the God of Life. Instead, God puts death's rejection right on Cain's forehead. With God's mark, Cain remains alive by God, even as he goes away from the presence of God. Here is God, ever sticking with it.

If you've read *The Scarlet Letter*, you know the story of Hester Prynne, who is condemned to wear a scarlet "A" on her chest as punishment for her adultery, and her unwillingness to divulge the name of the man with whom she had the affair. Hester's scarlet letter is a powerful symbol of the role of shame in our society. For the townspeople of seventeenth-century Boston, Hester's act of sin was the most important thing about her. The tragedy of the story is how her punishment keeps those around her guilty, rather than providing anyone with redemption. The two men in her life are both driven to ruin by it, and the townspeople remain trapped in self-righteous judgment.

Cain's mark is not Hester's scarlet letter. God does not condemn Cain to wander the world bearing an "M" so that everyone will always know what he did to his brother. He is marked instead with protection, so that no one will bring him harm. Can you imagine? We live in a society that busily cuts out red letters for everyone, but we are loved by a God who would never make us wear them. God has far more grace for humanity than we have on ourselves.

Though Cain is not his brother's keeper, God is Cain's. And while original sin wants to mark us all with the scarlet letter "S," original blessing marks us with nothing less than the faithful love of God.

Rain on the Just and the Unjust

What drives Cain further east of Eden? What is the sin that casts him out? Cain resents God's favor of Abel so much he kills him for it. He is more than willing to accept God's blessing for himself, but he resents God giving blessing to anyone else.

As I mentioned at the very beginning of the book, there is a cost to living out our blessing, and that is to see the world as God sees the world. When we accept blessing, we also accept we are all connected to God, and we are all connected to each other and to creation. We are our brother's keeper and our sister's keeper and our earth's keeper.

We cannot expect God to rain down blessings on us while we curse others, or worse, while we ask God to curse others. As Jesus said at the end of his Sermon on the Mount,

> "You have heard that it was said, 'You shall love your neighbor and hate your enemy.' But I say to you, Love your enemies and pray for those who persecute you, so that you may be children of your Father in heaven; for he makes his sun rise on the evil and on the good, and sends rain on the righteous and on the unrighteous."[2]

Scripture is replete with the message of love and care for others. When a man asks, "Who is my neighbor?" Jesus responds with the story of the good Samaritan. When a rich man asks what he must do to fulfill the law and the prophets, Jesus tells him to sell all he has and give it to the poor. Jesus tells us whatever we do to the least of these, we do to him.

2. Matthew 5:43–45.

Jesus dines with tax collectors and speaks to outcasts because Jesus sees every last one of them as God's beloved, as blessed and endowed with the unshakeable image of God. In other words, he sees them for who they really are, and not as the letter we stitch onto their chests.

It may be the most difficult thing about original blessing to accept how lavishly God bestows it. I'm reminded of the parable of the workers in the vineyard, which I call the anti-American parable because it's so offensive to the way we understand the world. A landowner goes out and hires some workers for the day, and he tells them he will pay them a denarius, which was a day's wages. A few hours later, he goes out and hires some more, and he hires a few more several hours after that. The landowner does this throughout the day, up until the eleventh hour. At quitting time, he comes to pay all of the workers, and he gives each of them a denarius. Well, the men that had been working all day are just furious. "We've been out here all day!" they complain. "Why do these other workers get paid the same amount as we do?" And the landowner replies, "Didn't you agree to work for the day for one denarius? I'm not doing anything wrong by you. Don't I get to do what I want with what's mine? Or is your eye evil because I am good?"

When I read that last verse, I think of Cain, whose resentful eyes reject the goodness of God when it is directed anywhere other than himself. God's blessing is not fair. It is a gift. And who are we to say what God does with God's goodness?

What's saddest to me about Cain is that he is not lacking anything. God does not look unfavorably upon Cain, just on his offering. Cain still lives in the presence of God, in the fertile land God created, and as a child endowed with God's image. What does he have to be so upset about? I think it wasn't enough for Cain to be beloved. He also wants to be special, or in the word used in Genesis, favored. And those are different things.

Thank God, I'm not writing a book about favor, because it's a mystery to me as much as it is to you. But blessing and favor could not be more different. Favor implies you have done something to warrant God's extra attention, or at the very least that you believe you have God's attention in some form or fashion that is different than other people. Favor is very near favoritism, and it's so alluring to imagine ourselves in that select camp. We can begin to come up with very detailed schemes of God guiding the minutiae of our lives because of our faithful service. But it's a terrible trap. When we ground our entire identities in the shifting sand of our own actions, as if we have control over God's blessing or God's favor, as if we can win God over to our way of thinking, we may as well just go back to grounding our identities in the shifting sand of our own sinfulness. At some point, that house is going to fall. A loved one is not going to get better. We are going to lose the job. Our child is still going to be addicted. And then we're left bereft, wondering what we did to lose God's grace. But God isn't running a varsity sports team where we get cut when we don't perform up to standards. God is on our team, even when the world seems intent on our defeat.

Of the billions of people in the world, I know I'm not

all that remarkable. And that's fine. Not everyone can make history or stand out on a grand scale. This is something our culture of instant celebrity could probably stand to learn. Specialness is not everything, even if we live in a society that makes it seem that way. And specialness is not blessing. Special relies on you. Blessing comes from, relies on, and echoes back to God. I don't think God cares that much about specialness. If anything, scripture shows us that God chooses people who everyone else thought were anything but special. Special people can make us feel impressed, but they also can make us feel depressed. Blessing only makes us feel loved. Special simply doesn't happen to just anyone. Blessing simply happens for everyone.

Cain's big pitfall, his critical error, is that he wants to be favored, to be special, so badly, he forgets he is blessed.

So, when I say original blessing is a matter of life and death, I also mean it quite literally. When Cain loses his connection to blessing, and when he rejects the blessing of his brother, his heart turns violent and his hands become covered in blood. Cain mistakes his offering for his personhood. He confuses favor for blessing. He loses his anchoring in the steadfast blessing of God, and he and Abel both pay for it dearly.

The blessing of God is not special. It is universal. But there is beauty in that, because it binds us to one another in a way specialness never could. To receive original blessing is to be drawn into love for our brothers and sisters, love for our neighbors, love for our enemies, and yes, love for ourselves. Even when we don't feel special.

Timshel

The story of Cain and Abel is a story about blessing. And it is not a story about murder as much as it is a story about how murder can be prevented.

In John Steinbeck's novel *East of Eden*, Adam Trask and his two sons, Aron and Cal, learn in time that Cathy, their wife and mother, has abandoned them to run a brothel. (And yes, the names Adam, Cal, and Aron are meant to parallel Adam, Cain, and Abel.) Cal, who is more vindictive and cunning than his angelic brother, also feels like the less favored son. He becomes despondent, believing that he has inherited a sinfulness from his mother he cannot escape. But the Trask housekeeper, Lee, tells Cal the story of Cain and Abel. Lee has spent hours pondering the story, and keeps coming back to one word: *timshel*. In Hebrew, timshel can mean either "you must" or "you may." Lee wonders whether God told Cain he must rule over sin, or only that he may. Is it a command, or a declaration, or simply the presentation of a choice? Regardless, he tells young Cal that God gives each person the freedom to choose what to do, and that he is not destined to follow in the footsteps of his mother. Years later, when Cal asks for his father's blessing as Adam lies on his deathbed, Adam speaks his final word: *timshel*.

Steinbeck's novel heartbreakingly explores what it means to feel stalked by sin, and the legacy of sin. Like a hungry animal crouching at the door waiting to attack, each of us must—or may—rule over sin. That this admonition from God comes so quickly on the heels of the man and the woman leaving the garden is a strong reminder that we have no excuses to turn away from God. We cannot fall back on some idea of a sin nature to blame for what we choose, nor should we let our sins or the sins of others incapacitate us from seeking the way of God. We are not children anymore, and we must confront a world where sin is both a viable and an often-attractive option. If we do well, we will find the path toward wholeness. If we don't do well, we only step closer toward a sin that desires to strike us.

If we want to do well, we are at our best when we dwell in blessing. Blessing is what keeps us out of the rat race of what some call works righteousness, the feeling that we must earn our oxygen usage and counteract the things we've done wrong. But that's not doing well. That's just doing. Anne Lamott remarked once that many people want her to be a human doing instead of a human being, and we know exactly what she means. When our actions don't find connection to our souls in a meaningful way, when we are doing things out of guilt or duty and not joy or purpose, we are not doing well. We are just stuck in a pattern of doing, desperate to prove our worth. But blessing reminds us we do not need to prove our worth, because it rests safely in God. Doing well is an act of living in the grace that surrounds us in such a way that we can not only rest in it but send it forward.

Doing well is another way of saying that we gain wisdom. When we do well, we show our ability to discern how we respond to our knowledge of good and evil. Proverbs 15:2 says "The tongue of the wise dispenses knowledge, but the mouths of fools pour out folly." The word for "dispense" is the same as "do well" in Genesis 4. If you've ever seen one of those old coin dispensers at cash registers, you've watched as the cashier inputs your cash and then the dispenser spits out your change in a little silver bowl. The dispenser knows how much to keep, and how much to let go. As we take in knowledge of both good and evil, we have to decide what's worth keeping and what needs to be let go. And, as the proverb says, the wise person speaks only what makes the cut, while a fool's mouth cascades words without discretion. If we do well with knowledge, we enhance it to become wisdom. If we don't, we become foolish and stupid. When we confront this question grounded in blessing, we find ourselves more intentional about what to keep, and more free about what and when to let go.

When we read further into the story, we find a parallel between God's admonition to Cain in Genesis 4 and Moses' admonition to the Israelites in Deuteronomy 30. Moses says,

> This commandment that I'm giving you right now is definitely not too difficult for you. It isn't unreachable. It isn't up in heaven somewhere so that you have to ask, "Who will go up for us to heaven and get it for us that we can hear it and do it?" Nor is it across the ocean somewhere so that you have to ask, "Who will cross the ocean for us and get it for us that we can hear it and do it?" Not at all! The word is very close to you. It's in your mouth and in your heart, waiting for you to do it.[3]

Just as sin is waiting for you, crouching at the door, the word is also waiting for you. But it does not have to knock or crouch, for the word is already very close to you. It's in your

3. Deuteronomy 30:11–14, CEB.

mouth and in your heart. The word of God is very close to us, while sin must always stalk us at a distance. Sin is waiting for us, but it is our choice whether we open the door. Blessing is not waiting for us, because blessing is already with us and within us, regardless of whichever side of the door we're standing. Blessing is the home, and sin is the stranger. And how much closer it is for us, now that the Word has become flesh and dwelt among us full of grace and truth. The word is waiting for us, and the Word is waiting for us. In our mouth and in our hearts, abundant life awaits.

As Moses continues his rallying speech to the Israelites, we hear echoes of themes we've discussed throughout this book. He announces,

> Look here! Today I've set before you life and what's good versus death and what's wrong. If you obey the Lord your God's commandments that I'm commanding you right now by loving the Lord your God, by walking in his ways, and by keeping his commandments, his regulations, and his case laws, then you will live and thrive, and the Lord your God will bless you in the land you are entering to possess. But if your heart turns away and you refuse to listen, and so are misled, worshipping other gods and serving them, I'm telling you right now that you will definitely die. You will not prolong your life on the fertile land that you are crossing the Jordan River to enter and possess. I call heaven and earth as my witnesses against you right now: I have set life and death, blessing and curse before you. Now choose life—so that you and your descendants will live—by loving the Lord your God, by obeying his voice, and by clinging to him. That's how you will survive and live long on the fertile land the Lord swore to give to your ancestors: to Abraham, Isaac, and Jacob.[4]

4. Deuteronomy 30:15–20, CEB.

Life and death. Blessing and curse. Fertile land given to us by God. We have heard this before, and we will continue to hear it again and again. A generative relationship with God finds us both resting in blessing and pursuing life. When we turn away from blessing, we turn our hearts away from life. And as Cain reminds us, turning away from life affects far more than just us.

Integrating Our Inclinations

As humans, we only have two basic problems. We don't know what to do with our blessing, and we don't know what to do with our sin. Other than that, life is pretty straightforward.

As we learn to navigate the knowledge of good and evil in this fertile land east of Eden, we can center our quest around two questions:

How do I find the blessing of God that I may live in harmony?

What do I do about the dis-harmony I experience with God, myself, and others?

According to Jewish tradition, within each of us resides an inclination for good, the *yetzer hatov*, and an inclination for evil, the *yetzer hara*. They are both necessary, but each must be directed to serve the grand intent, which is a harmonious life with God, others, and ourselves. We can also call this way of life shalom, or wholeness. The word *yetzer* means to fashion or create, so imagine the *yetzer hara* and *yetzer hatov* as two hands guiding clay on a pottery wheel, forming and reshaping it daily by the rhythms and choices of our lives. Our human nature is not static, but dynamic. It is not iron but clay.

With descriptions like good inclination and evil inclination, it's easy for us to moralize them almost immediately, or to pit one against the other. But they are more complex than that, and they aren't to be battled against each other but complemented with one another. We can call the good inclination conscience, and the evil inclination drive. Since the goal is wholeness, we would be incomplete without them both. In fact, a well-known Jewish commentary asserts that when God surveyed creation and said, "It is good, it is very good," the conscience was the "good" and the drive was the "very good."[5] Human agency is what makes our relationship with God worth having, even if it's the very thing that makes it most complicated.

The yetzer hatov, what we'll call conscience, is tasked with guiding us toward the good. We can also see it as our natural desire for virtue, our inclination toward God. If the drive is fire, the conscience is water. It can subdue flames that threaten destruction, and bring a calming, restorative voice to our intentions.

But people with too much conscience are insufferable. They don't enjoy life because they're too busy moralizing everyone and everything around them. They're the nagging tattle-tales. They can take the air right out of a party. If you think of all the religiously upright who got so bothered by

5. Genesis Rabbah 9:7.

Jesus having dinner with tax collectors, you get the picture. It's ironic to realize that the religious are sometimes like this, but God never has been.

The yetzer hara, what we'll call drive, is like our survival instinct. We could also call it desire, or ambition. It is a driving force, the part of our human will that often gets things done. We literally cannot live without it. Without drive, we would be listless and apathetic, and we wouldn't strive for anything. A survival instinct is connected to a love for life and a desire to keep it. Only when drive runs the show or goes unchecked does it become evil.

Desire itself is not sin. Rather, sin is misplaced desire, or overemphasized desire. Natural hunger becomes gluttony. Sexual longing turns into objectification. Motivation for success becomes ruthless ambition. The answer isn't to rid yourself entirely of any of these things, and it isn't helpful to label these impulses as bad, either, but to realize you've become imbalanced in your response to them.

Desire is not evil; what matters is the source of desire and the direction and intensity with which we seek it. And we need to remember there is such a thing as too much conscience, too. I've all too often seen the inclination to do good bring someone to the brink of exhaustion and burnout. Without our desire for self-preservation, we cannot live sustainably as doers of justice and seekers of peace.

Jewish tradition says a person is born with drive and gains conscience after turning thirteen, which is the age of maturity. Although I find it a better metaphor to possess both human inclinations from day one, I do appreciate the symbolism implied, and the push toward growing up and becoming responsible. A thirteen-year-old, as an adult in the eyes of the temple, now must begin the work of mature faith. And that work is to balance even an inclination that might pull toward sin.

The Talmud, a Jewish collection of rabbinical commentary and discussion, says the Torah is the antidote, the healing medicine to teach how to integrate both conscience and drive. One verse says, "If you toil in Torah you will not be handed over into his hands,"[6] and the "his" is drive. The Talmud uses the word "toil" on purpose here. Just as Adam toils in the fertile land and Eve toils in childbirth, we are to toil in following the commandments of God. This is the work that brings life. And in that work, we are capable of living into our conscience and not living in fear of our drive.

I actually wonder if we could see the story of Jesus' temptation in the wilderness as a kind of yetzer hara drive story, a parable of how Jesus integrated his drive in a way that would bring wholeness and life. When faced with the inclination to demand life from even a stone, Jesus refrains. When faced with the inclination to seize power and authority, Jesus refrains. When faced with the inclination to receive favor from God or to test God, Jesus refrains. Instead, Jesus turns his drive toward more purposeful ends. When he heals, he remembers why. When he preaches, he remembers what for. When he is met with favor, he usually slips away into the crowd, or urges the person to keep the

6. Talmud, tractate Kiddushin, 30b.

miracle under wraps. Jesus is not controlled by his drive. He channels his drive toward fulfillment of God's kingdom. When he sets his face toward Jerusalem, he is determined, but he remembers who he is, and what he values. Jesus' drive sustains him through his Passion. His conscience sustains his calling, and his posture, and his forgiving response on the cross. Without them both, we would have no Easter. Perhaps this is one of the many ways we can peer into the mystery of the incarnation.

We carry with us both the instinct to survive and the instinct to be virtuous. There's a sanity and a simplicity when we see our human nature this way. We are not all bad, or all good. At any given time, we are tipping toward one scale or the other, and we have multiple scales going at the same time. We might be doing wonderfully well in one area of our lives, while we are royally botching things elsewhere. There's no balancing of the scales, but that's okay. Our goal isn't balance. It's integration.

One of my yoga teachers used to walk around the class reminding us that our flexibility and balance are different from side to side and different from day to day. I like to think of that as a gentle reminder not only to be kind to myself on the days when I fall over most of the class, but also to think humbly of myself on the days when my poses are strong and centered. It's a reminder that I'm not all good at yoga, and I'm not all bad at yoga. I practice yoga, and I do my best. I think that's what it means to live with conscience and drive. We find wholeness not outside of our inclinations, but only when we breathe through the ups and downs that come from within them. But we don't want to spend any time on either end of the spectrum, whether it's the selfishness of drive or the selflessness of conscience. Too much of either of them, and we're off balance.

If we see drive as a longing for aliveness, and conscience as a longing for faithfulness to God, when they are combined we become alive to God and in God and with God. We are not saintly robots who follow after God because we haven't considered any other path. We aren't condemned humans doomed to walk only the path of sin. We are free human beings who follow God when faced with every path. We become wise, because we know true aliveness does not happen unless we align ourselves with God. I believe this is at the very heart of the divine mystery: God has created us in God's image, so that we may freely choose God with fidelity as God freely chooses us with fidelity. As image-bearers, we are caught up in the very fidelity of God that precedes us. In our better moments, we, too, are people who are sticking with it.

Resting in Blessing

If we return to our image of the glass as our relationship with God, we remember that the contents can be half full, half empty, cloudy, or crystal clear. Our relationships in the world and with the world are constantly swirling and changing. If we rely on them to be the basis of our identity, or the center of our stability, or even the framework by which we see the world, we will be tossed around mercilessly by our ever-shifting feelings and a world we cannot control. Cain became caught up in the swirl of the contents and lost sight of the reality of the glass. He doubted his belovedness, and he resented the belovedness of Abel.

So we return to the words God spoke to Cain: "Sin is crouching at the door; its desire is for you, but you must master it." How? The mastery lies not in crouching but in resting. As counterintuitive as it may seem, we do not strike back first. We rest first in blessing. We ground ourselves in the space of God. We remember we are enveloped by a relationship with God that isn't going anywhere. And then we look with wiser eyes to find a path that will guide us toward life.

Sin crouches, but we rest. I remember as a child finding it so strange that Psalm 23 describes God as preparing a table before us in the presence of our enemies. Who wants to eat in front of her enemies? I couldn't imagine it would make for an enjoyable dinner. But when I think about resting in blessing, it now makes sense. Sin crouches. Our enemies stand over us. But we are just fine, resting here in the arms of God's blessing. We can pass the potatoes and sip our wine. Our enemies may stand nearby, but they cannot take away our blessing. We may find that we feel more capable of mastering sin when we reside peacefully in blessing. Surely goodness and mercy will follow us all the days of our life, and we will dwell in the house of the Lord forever.

We're Blankets, Not Sheets of Steel

When Isaac Newton was trying to explain and understand gravity, he described space as static and flat. If an object didn't have anything in its way, it would naturally move in a straight line at a constant speed. When Einstein came up with his theory of relativity, though, he argued that space is not static or flat. Space is constantly in flux, and it curves around objects based on mass and energy. While Newton saw space like a flat sheet of steel, Einstein saw space like a blanket. If you put a weight on the steel, it doesn't budge. But put a weight on a blanket, and everything changes.

As it turns out, Einstein was right. In fact, the more we learn about the world, the more we realize there's only one constant in the whole universe: change.

When we think of the way we understand human nature, we're continually debating a similar kind of idea. Is it nature or nurture? Is it talent or practiced skill? In recent years, a number of scientists, psychologists, and sociologists have shown studies proving humans are far less determined than we tend to think. We are not human sheets of steel. We are far more like Einstein's blanket, curving around the weight of whatever forces we encounter. We are not static beings, but people constantly in action and reaction.

Plato scoffed in *The Republic* at the idea that an old man can learn new things, joking that he can no more learn much than run much. But we live in a world where no fewer than twelve octogenarians ran in the 2015 Boston marathon, so perhaps Plato underestimated them. As it turns out, humans are exceptionally pliable. While we used to think the brain stopped being capable of learning after a certain age, we now know that the human brain is capable of adaptation, no matter the age. And though the human body moves toward decay, we have also seen a compelling number of our elders show us that old bodies do not need to be weak and immobile. An old dog may be stuck in his old tricks, but he's not incapable of learning a new one.

Blessing Has Growth in Mind

As a parent, I've seen a veritable onslaught of advice in recent years on how it's actually not a good idea to tell your child she's smart, or a natural at art or lacrosse. It's a strange thing to hear after so many years of being encouraged to shower our children with an endless stream of self-congratulatory compliments. Surprisingly enough, it actually causes children to perform worse in the long run. A smart student now has something to lose, and feels pressure to keep it up, which ends up affecting her performance. Or a star athlete feels gifted, and consequently doesn't put in the same amount of time practicing as the other members of the team. Kids perform far better when they perceive themselves as adaptable, even if their current performance doesn't necessarily demand it. So instead of telling your child he's smart, it's much better to commend him for understanding that material, and applaud his efforts to listen in class and study it at home. He'll see his grade as a reflection not only of his intellect but also his effort, which is exactly what it is. Psychologists call this a fixed mindset versus a growth mindset.

A fixed mindset assumes a child is born with a certain level of capability, whether academic, athletic, or creative. If you're smart, you only have to ride the wave of your lucky DNA. If you're not smart, well, there's just not much you can do about it. A growth mindset, while acknowledging some natural limits, recognizes the remarkable range of potential available to everyone. With practice and effort, you wouldn't believe how much you can improve. If you're not good at something now, it doesn't mean you're doomed forever to be bad at it. You aren't a person who doesn't get any math, ever. You're just a person who doesn't get this math right now.

When you think about it, this makes perfect sense. No one gets motivated by a lost cause. Nobody wants to take on a project that is doomed to go nowhere. If someone told you you'd never improve at math, you would never bother with your algebra homework.

Original blessing is a growth mindset. Rather than dooming you to a static sin nature you have no ability to control much less change (talk about a fixed mindset), original blessing gently reminds you that God's mercies are new every morning. You have been given gifts and talents, to be sure, and you're called to use them. But more than anything, you have been given potential. Every morning, that potential awaits your movement.

I'm reminded of Jesus' parable of the sower who tossed seeds on a path, on rocky ground, among thorns, and on good soil. The seeds on the path were eaten by the birds, the seeds on rocky ground grew quickly but were just as quickly scorched by the sun. The seeds among thorns were eventually overtaken by them, and the seeds on good soil grew thirty, sixty, or a hundred fold. Each of the seeds carried the potential for life within them. None of the seeds were defective. But the potential of the seeds had to be received, and not just briefly, but deeply enough for them to take root and grow. Potential can be a spark that blooms into life, generating good things when properly nurtured. Or it can be a step that moves your feet along a path where your best gifts will be overgrown by thorns. But there's never any question of whether the seed has potential or not. A seed carries within it the promise of new life.

Though original sin has told us a story of being stuck in our sin, when we turn to scripture, we actually find a very different story. Though modern science has just come to realize how amazingly malleable people are, the wisdom of scripture has told us this all along.

What Does Sin Mean in Scripture?

Other than that awkward moment when you're reciting the

Lord's Prayer in church and you don't know whether to say debts or trespasses, sin is the word Christians universally use to describe any movement away from God. In English, sin is an all-encompassing word. It can mean stealing a candy bar or dropping the atomic bomb. It can be personal or communal. In cultural terms, it can even be religious or unreligious, connoting something that is simply seen as bad but doesn't necessarily relate to God. While it's pretty impressive to note the range of the word "sin," it has also caused problems as subtlety has gotten lost in translation. Much like the fabled tale of Eskimos having fifty words for snow, the Bible has far more than one word for sin. For us to get a clear picture of what we mean when we talk about sin, it's important for us to take these words and their contexts into consideration.

There are fifty different words for what we call sin in biblical Hebrew, which is the language of the Old Testament. Three of them account for the vast majority of verses. The most common, *hatta*, occurs 595 times and can be described as missing the mark. Like an archer aimed at a target, a *hatta* is an action or intention that did not hit the bull's-eye. The word *awon*, which is used 231 times, implies being twisted instead of straight, bent instead of upright. This is often translated "crooked." Lastly, the word *pesa*, used 136 times, means a willful violation of the law. It carries with it the connotation of rebellion, with political undertones. We could use the word "uprising" or the term "breach," either of a contract or a social norm.

When we turn to the New Testament, we see that Greek

also has a number of words we translate as sin, though only one is used in what could be considered a majority of settings. *Hamartia* is used 173 times. It is very near the Hebrew word *hatta*, and is similarly translated as missing the mark. In both the Greek and the Hebrew, missing the mark is not just about a target but more broadly about a relationship. To miss the mark is to have a falling out, or a drifting away. It describes a relationship that has been broken and will need to be mended. Hamartia literally comes from the combination of the words "not" and "a part." So *hamartia* also describes not being part of something, or being separated. When we miss the mark, we move away from God. To repent, then, is to live in God, and with God.

The second most common Greek word is *adikia*, which is used only twenty-five times. *Adikia* is most often translated as iniquity or unrighteousness. A judge who rules unfairly, or a person who cheats another person, would be guilty of *adikia*. There are also words for lawlessness or social chaos (*anomia*), a lapse or a turning away (*paraptoma*), irreverence (*asebia*), and walking in the wrong direction (*parabasis*), to name a few.

If you look over the list, they do not describe a state of sin in which people exist that drives their natures to evil. There's no fixed mindset at work. These words describe actions and choices, not the very nature of a person. And they can just as well describe the actions of a group, a community, or a society, which is important for us to remember. Not all sin is personal sin, even if that's the primary way we tend to think about it in our highly individualized view of society.

The most predominant word for sin in both the Hebrew and the Greek assumes in its very definition our ability to hit the mark. We can't miss the mark unless we assume the mark is where we're aiming, right? In 768 instances of the word "sin" in the Bible, we are described as people who are standing with a bow and arrow, aiming at a target that we miss. That's not a sin nature, and it's definitely not total depravity. That's novice, or perhaps distractedness, or bad aim. It could be any number of things. But the idea that we are not designed to hit the target set before us would be completely antithetical to the way sin is put forth in the vast majority of scripture.

When scripture calls us to goodness, to repentance, to grace, it's not like telling a fish to ride a bicycle. It's not something so contradictory to who we are and what we can do that it's an impossible notion. Salvation is available to us because God has offered it, but also because God has designed us to be capable of responding to it. We can take aim at the target simply because God chose to make us that way. Yes, we miss the mark. None of us gold medal in righteousness or goodness day after day. But that doesn't mean we are without any ability to play the game.

One Greek word on the list, *adikia*, tends to confuse us the most. It shows up a number of times in the book of Romans, and as I mentioned, it's usually translated as unrighteousness or iniquity. *Adikia* is often (and wrongly) used to define the idea of a "sin nature," but that isn't what it means. The context is far more interesting than that. Adikia is actually the name of a Greek goddess. She and her sister, Dike, are often depicted in art battling one another, though Dike always has the upper hand. Adikia is the goddess of injustice, and Dike is the goddess of justice. In classical Greek literature, their names became terms used to describe actions between people as either just or unjust. When the New Testament writers used these words, they added a new dimension, so that justice was not only what was right but specifically what was right in the eyes of God. Justice is the goal, or the target. Injustice is anything that points away from that target. With *adikia*, there is a sense in which a string of actions or decisions has resulted in a way of life, and it has become ugly. In fact, the goddess Adikia is actually portrayed as ugly in art, in comparison to the more beautiful Dike. Some may want to call that a sin nature, but it's different for at least two reasons. One, it's created and not inborn. It comes out of a long line of choices. Two, it's reversible. There's no sense in which anyone other than Adikia herself is condemned to be stuck in a pattern of injustice.

If you've ever read Oscar Wilde's brilliant novel, *The Picture of Dorian Gray*, you already understand how this happens. At the beginning of the story, Dorian Gray is a handsome and likable fellow, even if he's a little inclined to pride. As the story progresses, however, Gray's compounding bad choices begin to affect him, drastically altering how he perceives himself. By the end, he feels he's become unrecognizable to himself. He is no longer handsome or likable. He becomes overwhelmed by where he has let his life take him, and he struggles for a way to confront what he's become. Dorian Gray knows nothing of blessedness, so he's left with nothing but his shame. It's a heartbreaking story. It certainly shouldn't be anything like the Christian story we tell.

Sometimes people (and groups) get into patterns of behavior that can alter who they are. But there's still no need to call that an innate and unchangeable sin nature. We call them bad habits. And they can always be changed, even though it can be incredibly difficult to do so. Dike always stands over and above Adikia, even if the battle is lengthy and arduous.

Missing the mark, twisting something around, walking the wrong way: the Bible talks about sin as something that ought to be called out, but not something that ought to be condemning to the point of shame. In this list of words, sin is an action, a choice, or if we've made a number of them in a row, a path or a habit. There is nothing irreversible or determinate about it. Sin is not a state of being. It is a way of being in the world that is always and every moment in flux, based on our choices. It's a growth mindset, not a fixed one.

To put this another way, there is a difference between having fallen and being fallen. Sin (*hamartia*, *hatta*) means that we have fallen. It doesn't mean we *are* fallen. We may be in flux depending on our last action and our next intention, but we aren't simply tossed around on the waves of our own competence. We reside in the boat of blessed grace, which holds us steady even as we falter and sway from day to day. We may have fallen, but we *can* get up.

We All Live Downstream

A number of years ago, I read an article about the water supply in San Francisco. During a routine water testing, city officials realized, to their great concern, that city water showed traces of a number of drugs and pharmaceuticals. These drugs were not being entirely filtered by the standard process, which was designed to remove natural things like alkaline and dirt rather than heroin and Prozac. The result was a scary concoction, one that could prove lethal over time. Though not every resident of San Francisco had tossed leftover pills into the river or down the sink, everyone's water now carried traces of other people's addiction, depression, high blood pressure, insomnia, heart disease, cancer. The residents of San Francisco may have been treated as individuals, but the water told the story of a shared prescription. This deep connectedness is what led scientist and environmentalist David Suzuki to remark, "We all live downstream."

Living together as the family of God is beautiful, but it is also a profound responsibility, one we too easily remove from our shoulders. When we talk about sin, especially in the West, we tend to do so only thinking of ourselves. What counts as sin for me? How can I be healed of my own sin? When can I be forgiven? We spend far less time considering how what we do affects those far removed from us. How does my purchase of this clothing affect a woman in Cambodia? How does eating this fish affect the fisheries, not to mention the oceans? How does my long daily commute affect the air, and the price of oil (not to mention my quality of life!)? We shy away from these questions because they feel daunting and also impossible. But these questions are the other side of the coin of blessing. Our lives are connected, and we share across this wide planet the blessing of life in God. So we cannot live as islands unto ourselves, but are called to see each other instead as part of God's tapestry of creation.

I call this connectional sin. Connectional sin reminds us that our choices ripple out far beyond our own lives. Some have called it ancestral sin, but that feels too far away, as if it has something to do with people who lived long before me and are therefore not my problem. Connectional sin grounds us in our networked existence, and calls us to be mindful of how we weave this shared web. We are recipients of the problems we have inherited from those who have come before us, and we provide the legacy for those who will come long after us.

Perhaps the most harrowing example of this is a recent study done on the DNA of children of Holocaust survivors.[1]

---

1. Rachel Yehuda, Nikolaos P. Daskalakis, Linda M. Bierer, Heather N. Bader, Torsten Klengel, Florian Holsboer, and Elisabeth B. Binder, "Holocaust Exposure Induced Intergenerational Effects on FKBP5 Methylation," *Biological Psychiatry* (2015).

A Holocaust survivor's body responded to the stress of trauma and starvation by changing certain enzymes and proteins in the body. But those changes were then passed down to their children, whose own bodies then made reactive responses. The result is that children of Holocaust survivors are more susceptible to anxiety and PTSD. And so it is that one German dictator's sin can not only destroy an entire generation, but that generation's children and grandchildren. God, have mercy. We are far more connected than we know.

Just as there is no "outside" to our relationship with God, there is no "outside" of creation, either. When we say we throw something away, we have to admit on some level that we're lying. There is no away. There is only here. Again we lean on the wise words of David Suzuki: "The leading science corroborates this ancient understanding that informs us that whatever we do to our surroundings, we do directly to ourselves. The environmental crisis is a human crisis."[2]

Sin is always personal. It's just not only personal. What we do ripples out far beyond where we're standing. When we harm others by our choices, the consequences extend far beyond our walls. But the opposite is also true. When we choose life and live into grace and peace, light stretches further than our eyes can see.

There Is No "I" in Gospel

The truth is, sin in scripture is never only a matter of personal conscience. Sin is inherently relational, connecting us both

2. *Force of Nature: The David Suzuki Movie.* Entertainment One, 2012. DVD.

to God who calls us to an ethic of love, and to one another, with whom we are called to live as siblings of God's family. Sin is a communal reality. When we think of the Ten Commandments, we remember the first four describe our relationship with God, while the last six describe our relationship with others. When Jesus summed up all the law and the prophets, he emphasized the same relationality: love your God with all your heart, mind, soul, and strength, and love your neighbor as yourself. There's just no way to follow Jesus without being mindful of our neighbors.

I fear we've confused the personal nature of sin with an individualistic view of sin. Much of this stems from the doctrine of original sin, which slowly began to describe sin more and more as an individual problem. So it's important to remember that the concept of the modern human and even the modern individual conscience is a new idea, and we have to be careful not to assume that the writers of scripture understood sin in the same kind of overtly personal (and existential) way. Krister Stendahl once wrote a fascinating and controversial paper claiming that Protestant Christians have greatly misunderstood the way the apostle Paul treats sin. We read Paul, he said, "in light of (Martin) Luther's struggle with his conscience."[3] And of course, Martin Luther, the famous Reformer, began to approach sin that way because of Augustine, whose *Confessions* were, Stendahl contends, "the first great document of introspective conscience."[4]

3. Krister Stendahl, "The Apostle Paul and the Introspective Conscience of the West," *Harvard Theological Review* 56, no. 3 (1963): 199–215. *JSTOR*, 200.
4. Stendahl, "The Apostle Paul and the Introspective Conscience of the West."

When we read Paul assuming he has the mind of a twentieth-century Westerner, we can really botch things up theologically. Though it's true that sin, for Paul, was personal, it's contrary to his Jewish identity, and his understanding of the gospel, to assume he only approaches sin individually.

When we look to the Eastern church, who did not follow the West down our road of assertive individualism, we can clearly see the difference it's made in how they see sin. The Eastern church has no similar sense of individual conscience as the most important motivator or indicator. The people of God have a conscience. The body of Christ has a conscience. Your individual conscience just isn't the center of the universe in the life of the church, much less in the life of the world. That isn't to say it isn't important. It's just not the only show in town, much less the primary one.

If we look to our Jewish roots, we see the same communal emphasis. It's entirely contrary to Jewish thought to see repentance as something only done silently in a pew, whispering to God. Repentance is active, calling us not only to renounce our sinful action but also to repair whatever damage our action caused. Part of that is certainly asking God for forgiveness, but that isn't nearly all of it. On Yom Kippur, the Day of Atonement, the rabbi makes a point to remind the congregation that when you've committed sins against other people, God wants you to ask forgiveness from *them*, not just God.

Biblical repentance goes beyond asking God to wave a forgiveness wand over us. Andrew Park describes how our Western emphasis on *metanoia*, a Greek word meaning a cognitive regret, has far overshadowed the Hebrew word *shuv*, which sees repentance as active participation in justice. Repentance isn't simply asking God to fix our feelings, because whatever is wrong is about far more than just our emotions. It includes other people and relationships.

In Jewish tradition, *tikkun olam* is a phrase that means "repair the world." It's a calling to mend the brokenness we see all around us, whether we caused it or not. It's working together toward the goal of shalom, of wholeness. While Cain asked if he was the keeper of even his blood brother Abel, *tikkun olam* asks us to be keepers of all of humanity.

This can feel overwhelming, because it is. How can we try to clean up the messes of our neighbor when it's difficult enough to clean up the messes we make ourselves? But as with all things in God, there is grace here, too. While we are called to remember our connectedness, and therefore share in the responsibility of honoring others by our actions, we also remember that we are not the only people in the universe called to this work. When we lay down our rugged individualism, we not only realize we are not alone, but also that we can be supported by others around us. We don't have to do all the work. We aren't actually the saviors of the universe, thank God. We are simply asked to do the work we see in front of us, as we are able. Repairing the world doesn't demand us to be saviors; only participants.

Rat Park

In his book *Love and Hate*, ethnologist Irenäus Eibl-Eibesfeldt says humans are born with an innate drive to aggression, as well as an innate drive to social bonding. (The yetzer hara/drive and yetzer hatov/conscience described this long before his studies!) And although both are powerful, we are actually designed to respond first to social bonding. Eibl-Eibesfeldt calls this "cherishing behavior," the drive we have to see someone else and want to honor and care for them. That may sound obvious enough, but what's really interesting is that younger mammals have faces and features that encourage older mammals to see them in this way. Every puppy and kitten video circling the Internet should prove this point obviously enough. We are designed to want to love and care for our young. We're hard-wired to respond to them. Children make an extraordinary number of appeals to their caregivers, asking for contact and attention. It's only when a child's appeals go continually unanswered that the child becomes detached, less sociable, and potentially aggressive.

What's most interesting is that our drive to aggression or social bonding will lead us in different directions not based on our nature, but on our connections with those around us. For so long, we've seen sin as a moral failing (and sometimes it is) without wondering whether sin is also, and perhaps even more often, a social failing. What happens when someone's appeals for cherishing go consistently unanswered?

You may have heard of studies of drug addiction done on rats, where researchers placed a rat in a cage and gave it two water bottles. One was regular water, and the other was laced with cocaine. The rat continually returned to the cocaine water bottle, and would eventually kill itself with an overdose. One researcher, Bruce Alexander, wanted to know if the same thing would happen if the rat wasn't simply left in a cage by itself. So he built Rat Park, a community cage with tunnels and food and lots of rats living together. They, too, had both of the bottles, but the results were astonishing. The rats just weren't that interested in the cocaine. They tried it, but it didn't become an obsession. And unlike the solitary cage where all of the rats died, not one rat died from an overdose in Rat Park. And it isn't just rats. Johann Hari compared this data to Vietnam soldiers who became heroin addicts during the war.[5] Ninety-five percent of them simply stopped when they returned home. Her research led her to conclude, "The opposite of addiction is not sobriety. It is human connection."

When we don't feel grounded in love, whether by God or by those around us, we can potentially turn toward destructive connections instead. Drugs are one example, but humans are impressively creative in finding ways to connect. Our drive to social bonding will find an outlet somewhere, and it's not necessarily going to be in a place as safe as a loving parent.

What's most heartbreaking about this, though, is that we often treat negative behaviors like addiction in ways that only exacerbate the problem. We push people away at the moment they most need to be held and cherished. We instill a sense of shame in them, rather than enforcing a declaration of blessing. When we see sin only as a reflection of individual

5. Johann Hari, *Chasing the Scream: The First and Last Days of the War on Drugs* (New York: Bloomsbury, 2015).

morality, punishment seems the only fitting response. But aggressive or physical punishment creates distance, which only pushes someone further away from social bonding. Ostracism, shunning, solitary confinement, all of these merely degrade a person's foundation of care even further. And that isn't a sin we can only set on their shoulders. It's one we must shoulder ourselves, too. Punishment is a problematic reaction to social sin because it often serves as a form of scapegoating, where one person pays the penalty for the wrongs of a whole group of people.

I once heard Malcolm Gladwell speak about punishment and legitimacy.[6] He told us how when California wanted to get tough on crime, they instigated a "three strikes and you're out" rule. Basically, if you received three offenses of any kind, you would have to serve jail time. Twenty-five years later, California's crime rate hadn't gone down any more than states that didn't use any deterrents like three strikes you're out. The legislators behind the law were dumbfounded. Why didn't the threat of punishment work? If a leader or a society wants to be seen as legitimate, Gladwell said, you have to treat people with respect, act with fairness, and convey trustworthiness. Punishment doesn't fix a good number of problems because it threatens to undermine all three. It certainly undermines human connection.

In our eagerness to battle sin and fight crime, we've assumed that people are motivated most by fear and the threat of punishment. And the other assumption lurking underneath

6. Malcolm Gladwell, "Legitimacy." *www.Qideas.org*. Q Commons, 20 Apr. 2015. http://qideas.org/videos/legitimacy/.

it is the belief that people are also motivated to do the wrong thing. (There's original sin again.) But when we look at most recent studies, we see a different picture. People are most motivated by a desire to be loved and cherished. What we want most of all is not heroin but a home.

The Eyes Have It

As it turns out, the way we feel about ourselves is profoundly connected to the way we are seen by others. Stanford University did a study that revealed merely mentioning a stereotype to a group of minority students before taking a standardized test would negatively affect their test scores.[7] The same held true for a group of female students, who were told, for example, that boys tended to score better in math and science. Those female students did in fact score lower, while the female students who weren't told scored as well or better than their male counterparts. And there have been a number of other studies that show low-performing students who become honor society inductees with a simple change of environment. Beauty is indeed in the eye of the beholder. And we've often failed to recognize the power of our gaze on those around us. We need only remember what it feels like when someone turns away from us to realize that to avert our gaze from one another is truly sin.

When we return to the eyes of our first beholder, God, we also return to the eyes of love. We find the golden thread that guides us into life. To find our home in original blessing is

7. http://news.stanford.edu/pr/95/950816Arc5120.html.

to receive the steady gaze of the one who knows us best, and who loves us anyway.

In the same way God shines light on us by God's gaze, we can shed light on those we see around us. Our perception of others, and our reception of them, can either be isolating or life-giving. Even our eyes are designed to generate life.

When I was in college, my mom became very ill. She was in the hospital for months, and there was one nurse in particular that really rubbed her the wrong way. My mom, who likes just about everyone, couldn't stand this nurse. And here she was, captive under her care. It's not an experience any independent-minded person wants to have. One week, the doctors told my mom she was going to need a blood transfusion. She was so upset. Here was one more thing, and of course she would have no idea where this blood would be coming from. The transfusion worked well, though, and soon she was up out of bed and walking gingerly down the hall. As she looked up, who was coming her way but that nurse. My mom groaned inwardly. And then, in the very next moment, she said it was as if she felt God speaking right into her ear, saying, "Cynthia, give thanks for her. How do you know she wasn't the one who gave you her blood?" My mom felt that tough place inside her heart soften, and she found she could gaze with love at that nurse from then on.

It's a humbling thing to realize we are all connected. Often, we wish we weren't. We wish there wasn't a need for nurses and blood transfusions and people who come to bail you out of jail or rescue you when your car breaks down or pitch in to buy your dinner. We would rather be independent, and not have to show our needs like brightly colored patches on our sleeves. But life is not designed for us to live unto ourselves. We need each other, and we're connected to each other, whether we like it or not. We have patches of need all over us, but God has also given us a spool of golden thread so plentiful that it can reach across to others. The cost of blessing is to see the world the way God sees the world. And that means to see ourselves not against one another, but as our brothers' and sisters' keepers.

Bodies, Babies, and Baptism

One of the central problems with the doctrine of original sin is that it dramatically shifted our view of human sexuality. We cannot rethink sin, then, without addressing all the ways original sin has distorted our perspective. Once you believe we have a sin nature that is passed down from one generation to the next, procreation becomes a dangerous business.

When the man and the woman eat the fruit in the garden, they realize they are naked and clothe themselves. This one detail in the story has been used by many to malign human sexuality. (Talk about jumping to conclusions.) Of course, the Genesis 3 story alone is not the reason for Christianity's long history of disdain for sexual pleasure. Greek philosophers often spoke against the passions and many saw any human desire as sinful. When you add God and faith to that already common idea, it's a pretty powerful condemnation. Celibacy becomes the marker of true purity and holiness, and even Christian marriage is considered an unacceptable place for sexual enjoyment.

Though the text itself gives us no such details, many early church theologians described the garden of Eden as a sexually innocent place. Ambrose, the fourth-century archbishop of Milan, believed the garden was perfect, which he defined as entirely devoid of sex. He considered sexuality the worst sin of all, and chastity the only true way to return to a perfect state of righteousness. (Sorry, almost everyone in the world.) Third-century theologian Origen pointed out that marriage itself only came into existence after the fall, which he reasoned was due to its constant danger of sexual sin. The overarching consensus was that sex was necessary, but not necessarily good. It's a pretty reluctant view of sex. Sex has nearly always suffered from overly pessimistic views, again for reasons far too complicated to enumerate here. But these views became very specific as the doctrine of original sin developed.

Tertullian lived in Carthage around 200 CE. His theory, traducianism, which I call the doctrine of original sperm, claimed that sin is passed on from one generation to another through sex. More specifically, it's passed on through semen. (This is where we get the term "seminal identity.") He believed that all semen came from Adam (even *your* semen, male reader of today) because souls were created before the beginning of the world. And the souls are in the semen. This material soul transported all the male parts from one generation to the next. So sex was not only sinful, but the vehicle for all of human sin entirely.

The doctrine of original sperm paved the way for the theory that the virgin birth was necessary to keep sin from being passed on to Jesus. And it's one of the reasons the Roman Catholic Church ended up promoting the doctrine of perpetual virginity for Mary, even though scripture itself mentions that Mary and Joseph had children after Jesus was born.[1] If sexuality is impure, Mary cannot take part and still be considered the holy mother of God.

Augustine took Tertullian's doctrine of original sperm and pushed it even further. Because all the semen in the world was in Adam (bless his heart, or, as my friend said, bless Eve's), then all of humanity was present in the Garden. Because we all share in Adam's semen, we also share in Adam's punishment. This is the first attempt at a legal explanation of sin. We were present at the scene of the crime, so at the very least we're liable for accomplice charges. Augustine also described sin as a hereditary moral disability. We are born this way, he said, and we can't do anything about it. We just cannot choose the good any longer. This, of course, is the ground floor of what will become total depravity. And it comes through sex, because our guilt is inherited through the semen that began with Adam. As for sex in the garden, Augustine admits that had they not eaten the fruit, eventually sex would have happened for procreation reasons, but because the garden is perfect, it would not have been pleasurable.

Original blessing does not need to disparage human sexuality or marriage in this way. Like many things, sexuality can be both good and bad. But sexuality is part of creation, and God has not only blessed it but encouraged it. Sexuality

---

1. Matthew 13:55–56. Catholic theologians, among others, have argued that these children were Joseph's from a previous marriage, or cousins. Both are as much speculation as Mary's perpetual virginity.

brings life in a literal way, and it can also bring life to our relationships through intimacy and connection. Rather than seeing Adam and Eve as fallen when they began their family, we can see them as adults, or even simply as ready. They weren't living into their sin nature in intimacy. They were living into their human nature, and even did so within a covenant of fidelity.

Original blessing also honors abstinence and celibacy in a more holistic way. Rather than carrying the weight of all holiness, or the impossible standard of perfection, living without sexuality can be seen as simply a choice, and often an honorable one. It becomes a choice *for* something, rather than a denial of something, or some definitive way to maintain purity and holiness.

While original sin asks sex to carry the weight of the world, original blessing can approach sex with far more perspective and sanity. Sexuality is not bad, but it isn't everything, either. It is one part of the human experience, and is to be given its healthy and rightful place.

In a broader sense, original blessing carries a far greater opportunity to respect and value our bodies, rather than contribute to a culture of shame, self-denial, self-abasement, and negative body image. If we are taught to see our bodies as the source of our sin nature, it's not particularly easy to appreciate them, much less to know what to do with them. When we believe our bodies are created good, we can choose to live into them as a natural part of human life blessed by God.

Though we have much to do to disentangle the convoluted

messages Western Christianity has sent about human sexuality and the body, original blessing provides us with a healthy starting place, and a holistic foundation. We can see sexuality as simply what it is, a natural part of life, and not the act upon which the morality of the cosmos rests. When we remove sex from this strange prison-pedestal, we may find we are able to approach it as a gift rather than a curse, and perhaps even treat it more reverently.

Blessings Come in Small Packages

When sin nature is passed on through procreation, it opens up a number of perplexing questions about babies, too. The first and most obvious is the question of whether babies are born sinful. My sweet friend Susan comes from a hardy Dutch Reformed family. She told me that when her grandmother came to visit new grandbabies in the hospital, she would cuddle them and say, "Ooooh, you're such a little sinner!" I can't say I'd ever heard the word "sinner" used as a term of endearment before that.

In 1740s New England, Episcopalian John Taylor and Presbyterian Jonathan Edwards exchanged a number of letters in local papers on the subject of original sin and infant baptism.[2] The debate was raging at the time, and the letter exchanges became quite heated, with Taylor arguing that it is unfounded to claim that we are sinful from birth, and Edwards arguing that we can rely only on God's grace to save

---

2. H. Shelton Smith, *Changing Conceptions of Original Sin: A Study in American Theology since 1750* (New York: Scribner, 1955).

us from our innate evil. When it was all said and done, Taylor finally got to the big question: Can Edwards really believe a newborn baby was destined to burn in eternity in hell unless baptized? At the time, infant mortality rates were quite high, and many babies died at birth, so this was by no means a hypothetical, abstract debate. Edwards answered yes. If the baby died before a baptism could be performed, the baby's sinfulness would be condemned by an eternity in hell.

There were no more letters exchanged after that. Either you can find reasoning behind that answer, or you can't.

If you adhere to the doctrine of original sin, you acknowledge all humans are born sinful. But most of us would find it difficult to explain where we see babies sinning. And while it may have made sense to attribute morality to babies in the fifth or fifteenth century, nowadays if you hear a parent saying how selfish and rude her colicky baby is, you know she's joking. (Or, you certainly hope so.) We remember that sin in scripture is most frequently described as an action that misses the target despite our aim. Babies are reflexive, reactive creatures. They don't aim. They don't even know about the target. They only know what they need, and they're right to cry when their needs aren't met. Crying, or whining, or even throwing a tantrum is not a sin. It is an appeal to their caregiver.

This debate about the sinfulness of babies led to a conversation about the age of accountability. People debated what age a child becomes morally responsible. If there is innocence, is there an expiration date? That creates a terrible predicament when growing up becomes synonymous with becoming sinful, or worse, becoming evil or damned. And though parents may feel "evil" is an appropriate description of their burgeoning teenagers, I hope we can all agree it's not the healthiest parenting approach to blame all of their angst on a sin nature that's kicking in. If we see growing up as a natural part of life, we can see teen questions and struggles as the necessary road toward maturity, not the road paved to hell.

The exchange between Taylor and Edwards epitomizes the extremes to which the doctrine of sin leads us. Edwards refused to back down or reconsider, because he was cornered by his conviction that God's grace had to work within a framework of total need at the expense of human goodness. (Talk about an addiction to an extreme makeover.) Taylor found himself arguing more and more forcefully for an idealistic view of human nature as a response.

Again we find ourselves in need of a return to sanity and simplicity, and in need of rejecting both unhelpful extremes. If we see babies as born with a human nature, we recognize quite naturally that they will exhibit both goodness and failure, to varying degrees. They possess a developing moral capability, one that is present when they are born and which becomes more complex and necessary as they grow. We don't need to see them as perfect or sinful, but as people growing and changing every day, just like the rest of us. Growing up is not a condemnation, but an opportunity to continually fulfill the potential we have to become participants in the life of God. Growing up brings complexity, but it doesn't have to bring condemnation.

Instead of worrying about the eternal fate of our newborns, we can welcome them as blessings.

Jesus implored the children come to him, for the kingdom belongs to them. And he also called us to become like little children before we can enter the kingdom of heaven. Jesus doesn't disparage children and certainly doesn't condemn them, but celebrates and honors them. And though they are not perfect any more than the rest of us, they are loved and welcomed with open arms.

Wade in the Water

When you change your view of one thing, you can watch it ripple out to a number of other things by extension. When original sin was pegged on human sexuality, it not only affected the way to receive and respond to children, but it also changed the understanding of the rite of baptism. Baptism is the first sacrament of Christianity. By Jesus' example, we enter into the waters of baptism as his followers. Though the rite itself has undergone numerous iterations in the past two thousand years, it has always been seen as a symbolic death and rebirth. (Once again, death and life are a major framework through which we understand our faith.) In the early church, people underwent a grand process of preparation and entered into baptism with awe and great thanksgiving. Through baptism, they declared their participation in the family of God. As Christianity became a more stable presence, baptism was seen as a family affair. Just as the New Testament describes whole families being baptized together, Christian parents baptized their children as an act of family faithfulness.

In both instances, baptism was understood to be an act of God conferring grace. It was a symbol of our acceptance to enter into God's covenant faithfulness, of our affirmative response to being brought into the family of God. Whether through parents on behalf of a child or through a person on her own behalf, baptism is one of the ways we participate in the life of God. We are buried with Christ, and raised to walk in new life. So baptism is an act, but at heart it is a blessing. It's an outward sign of our understanding of God's steadfast faithfulness to us. In baptism, we receive new life, which includes the remission of sins.

As the doctrine of sin gained prominence, once again the boxes of sin and death were swapped. Baptism came to be seen not as a movement toward life but as a solution for sin. And because your eternal destination hinged on whether you had been baptized or not, the church had a reason to strongly encourage everyone to take part. So baptism went from being understood as a covenant blessing to being a preventative measure. Rather than a move toward life, it was an act of avoiding punishment.

But baptism is meant to be seen through the lens of covenant faithfulness. Just as the prophets called God's people to repent and return to God, John the Baptist called people to repentance and invited them to enter new life in God. After the gift of Easter, we see this invitation not only as life in God, but also participation in Christ. We become brothers and sisters in God's family. So baptism is not about sin cleansing alone, and it isn't a get-out-of-hell card. It is a move toward life. In baptism, we vow to stick with God as a response to God always sticking with us.

A few years ago on Easter, my daughter was baptized. I was pastor at the time, and we held our Easter-morning gathering in my backyard. Our pool is a small rectangle, and as my daughter and I stepped into the water and took our place, we were surrounded by friends and loved ones on all sides. It was such a holy moment, not only because I was baptizing my daughter, but because her baptism was such a beautiful expression of what it means to be born into the family of God. Surrounded by people who love you, who will even make a vow to support and encourage you as you walk in the ways of Jesus, is a blessing indeed. She was ready to enter the waters of baptism that day, but she was ready because of the people who now encircled her around the edge of the pool. When she came up out of the waters and made her way back up the steps, they were waiting for her, literally with open arms . . . and a custom-designed towel for the occasion. Baptism is so much richer than sin cleansing or a religious requirement. It is a sacrament because it is the ritual act of being born anew into God's family.

When we see baptism as sin solution, we also lose the gritty reality that baptism is meant to signify death as a necessary part of our rebirth. As Jesus said, whoever wishes to save his life will lose it, and whoever loses his life for Christ's sake will find it. The martyrs of the early church considered baptism to be the first step of courage in deciding how they would respond to the empire. Because they had already chosen to die, the empire had no control or power over them. Though this is an extreme example, there's something inherent in the gospel that requires us to face our own death. As we follow Jesus, who set his face toward Jerusalem, we realize that we can only follow him courageously when we move beyond fear of death and into trust in life. If we remember that the knowledge of good and evil can also be described as the realization of our mortality, baptism is the way we courageously confront our mortality face to face. Once we accept that death is a natural part of living, we can also become open to the possibility of new life on the other side. In baptism, we participate in this mystery. We find our deepest courage when we realize God's love stays with us even to the grave. When we see baptism through the lens of life and death, we acknowledge that God is with us in our death, and God is with us beyond our death. In baptism, we participate in the faithfulness of God, who leads us into eternal life.

An Embodied Faith

Rather than distancing ourselves from human sexuality, the innocent wonder of babies, or even the unruly ups and downs of teenagers, original blessing invites us to enter into each stage and aspect of human life as a gift. As we follow an embodied Savior, we remember that flesh and blood is interwoven into the very fabric of life in Christ. We do not need to become less human to follow Jesus, but more fully human, embodying both the image and likeness of God.

IV. Rediscovering Jesus

Why Do We Need Jesus?

Now that we've unstitched and restitched a good portion of our theological blanket, it's time to return to the elevator with my new priest friend, who had just confirmed I don't believe in original sin and who then asked, "Then why do we need Jesus?"

I smiled and replied, "Brother, if you don't know why we need Jesus apart from original sin, it's time to go read the gospels again."

This may be one of the most tragic results of the doctrine of original sin. It deeply diminishes Jesus. When we emphasize sin as the big problem, and we make salvation the debt paid for our sin problem, then Jesus becomes not a savior but a sin portfolio manager. He is relegated from bread of life to debt officer. When we focus on sin, we also invariably begin to focus on punishment. Salvation becomes the way we get out of our punishment, rather than the way God restores us to fullness of life.

When sin is defined as the big problem, Jesus is necessary only insofar as he fixes it. How tragic to reduce so much beauty from the life of Jesus. If we only need Jesus for a blood debt transaction, we begin to wonder whether it was really necessary for him to teach us anything at all, or heal anyone, or show us another way to live. Why did he spend three years traveling and teaching if all we needed was for him to walk into Jerusalem and offer himself up for slaughter? This is what led evangelical pastor and sociologist Tony Campolo to call some people "vampire Christians, who only want Jesus for his blood." We lose so much when we see sin as the big problem. We lose the beautiful, wise, faithful life of Jesus himself. Even people who don't call Jesus Savior honor his life and teachings more than that.

If you compare art and liturgy from the first thousand years of Christian history to the second, the dramatic shift in our story about salvation is readily apparent. For the first nearly thousand years of Christian history, the crucifixion was not a central focus; Easter was. The cross was remembered one day a year, and the other three hundred and sixty four days were devoted to Easter. Symbols of Jesus as healer, life-giver, shepherd, light, and gardener populated art, houses of worship, liturgy, and prayers.[1] When we think about how the Western church's description of salvation was shifting, this makes perfect sense. When salvation becomes a form of payment, devotional focus turns primarily (and sometimes exclusively) toward the dying Jesus, who pays the price. Jesus never showed up bloodied on a cross in our art until we decided original sin required it of him.

1. Rita Nakashima Brock and Rebecca Ann Parker have written extensively on this matter in *Saving Paradise: How Christianity Traded Love of This World for Crucifixion and Empire* (Boston: Beacon, 2009).

It is startling and remarkable to consider that the first thousand years of Christian art depicted scenes of paradise and not crucifixion. It's even more shocking to realize that for the early church, paradise was described not as a separate heaven or a world to come, but as this world, imbued with God's Spirit. Life in the risen Christ is paradise. It is abundant life in the here and now.

When we embrace original blessing, and we reorient our view of the gospel to a story about life, and not simply about personal forgiveness, we are able to rediscover Jesus as so much more than our ticket out of trouble. He is instead the Way into life, and the living example of God's Word of Life.

Jesus, the Great Physician

When we think of life, we think of health and wholeness. When we are healthy and happy, we possess joyful exuberance and vitality. That's why we describe someone with a passionate and bubbly personality as full of life, while we use the word "lifeless" when we think of tiredness, apathy, and isolation. When we understand sin in relation to life (and death), we can see why sin is often described in scripture as a sign indicating a need for healing. In Psalm 38, David cries,

> There is no health in my bones
>   because of my sin.
> For my iniquities have gone over my head;
>   they weigh like a burden too heavy for me.
> My wounds grow foul and fester
>   because of my foolishness; . . .

Sin attacks our health, like a wound that is a result of our foolish choices (and the foolish choices of others). It is a force that moves against the life we are given in God, and the new life we are offered in Christ. When these choices overrun us, we become imbalanced. We become ill. Seeing sin as a need for healing reminds us that brokenness is foreign to our bodies. Like an infection, it shows that something isn't working properly. So while original sin would say someone is bad, original blessing need only say something is wrong. Illness isn't meant to be our nature. Health is.

Physically, our bodies are designed with immune systems that are meant to fight off viruses, bacteria, and diseases. Our bodies have an internal alarm system to let us know when something has veered off course. When we receive these signs, we don't tell ourselves it's because we are rotten at our core. We take the signs for what they are: an indication that we need to realign our bodies back to health. We recognize disease and illness as counter to our natural intended state. Scripture even goes beyond this idea, describing abundant life not as simply the absence of disease, but a fully flourishing mind, body, and soul. This is the meaning of salvation, and also wholeness. It is the salve of God over the wounds in our bodies, hearts, and souls.

In the Gospels, Jesus' acts of healing always include far more than just physical restoration. It isn't by accident that Jesus heals those who have been ostracized or rejected from society. Illness creates distance, which is why it's a sign of death and not life. When we are ill, we are also isolated, avoided, and sometimes even feared. Jesus heals lepers, a blind man, and a bleeding woman in order to return them to abundant life, which includes full membership and acceptance in human community. Jesus is the divine healer, who restores them (and us) not only to health but to relationship, relieving pain and, even worse, isolation and rejection. Healing for Jesus is always salvation. It is always an act of bringing whole life. For this reason, the early church often described Jesus as the medicine of life and the Great Physician.

As the doctrine of original sin developed, the Western church began to move away from healing language and instead describe sin and salvation in legal terms. Sin ceased to be viewed as the natural state of our bodies gone awry, but instead an unavoidable part of our human heredity. But once sin is considered part of our inborn nature, there is no restorative medicine to heal us. Sin became separated from the very life that can heal it. What is now required is not whole-life salvation, but payment. With this view of sin, the Western church began to rely almost exclusively on legal metaphors in some of the New Testament letters to describe salvation. Eventually, legal debt and payment were the only dimension of salvation left in the West.

If you don't believe me, poll strangers on the street and ask them why Jesus died. Most would respond—regardless of religious category—that it was to pay for sin. But that's such a limited and limiting view of what happened on the cross. And it's not the only answer the earliest followers of Jesus would have given. But the legal metaphors that took over in the West gave us the basic individual salvation story we know so well: If each person is born with a sin nature, we are lawbreakers in the eyes of God, and we owe God payment for our wrongs. Unfortunately, because of how bad we are, we cannot pay this debt, so God pays it for us by exacting our punishment on Jesus instead.

There are a number of significant problems with this interpretation of the gospel story, not least of which is that Jesus himself does not speak of his death this way. Jesus doesn't say that God is angry, or that he is paying the price for our sin. When he predicts his death to his disciples, he tells them he must undergo suffering and be betrayed at the hands of humans. He doesn't speak of the cross as something to be settled between him and God, but something to be endured between him and humanity. Jesus experiences God-forsakenness not because of God but *for us*, so that no part of our human experience, even the most death-determined parts, would remain untouched by his resurrected life. Jesus entered into our suffering and death not to pay a price but to make a way. And that way leads us to whole, redeemed, abundant life.

I remember many hours in theology class in seminary debating the problem of God's justice being at odds with God's mercy, which seemed like such an odd conversation to have. As some understood it, God's justice demands payment, and God's mercy is not allowed to overcome it, because then God would somehow lose righteousness. God can't be unjust and let evil slide without payment. So Jesus has to die on a cross to pay our sin debt so that God could maintain God's own sense of justice. But God is not stuck inside a dilemma we created out of our preoccupation with our own sin. God's hand is not forced to reconcile a problem God never had in the first place. *God is not trying to figure out how to pay for our sin. We are trying to figure that out.*

We have no evidence that God's mercy was ever at odds with God's justice, either. God's mercy and justice are not at odds but in harmony, one always softening and sharpening the other. Mercy and justice, however, are both in service to the bigger picture, which is life in God. (There we go again, moving things out of the life box.) Or, we could also say, the love of God. God's love brings mercy and justice, because without either, we would have no life. And we wouldn't move toward life, either. To be sure, legal metaphors are used in scripture to describe what happened on the cross, and much deep symbolism resides in the rituals of sacrifice Jesus certainly engages in his actions. But when we extract these from the life box and attempt to see them on their own, we find ourselves in a far less healthy relationship with them. If we see Jesus' story only through the lens of a courtroom and a legal debt, God's love, mercy, and grace become more of a "phew" than a "wow." Justice and mercy are not forces of punishment. They are agents of healing. The same can be said for the cross, where we find not condemnation but resurrected life.

Paradise Found

In the Gospel of Luke, one of the criminals hanged beside Jesus asked him, "Jesus, remember me when you come into your kingdom." Jesus replied, "Truly I tell you, today you will be with me in paradise." We could spend our time parsing the details, attempting to understand what paradise is and where paradise is and how paradise operates, but our energies may be better served by simply saying Jesus promised life to that criminal on the cross that day. He promised not any kind of life, but life in God and with God, not unlike life in the garden.

The word "paradise" isn't used often in scripture, but it is repeated in Revelation 2:7, which says, "To everyone who conquers, I will give permission to eat from the tree of life that is in the paradise of God." If we see the life, death, and resurrection of Jesus as God's culminating work, we can proclaim that the process of redemption begun in the garden culminates on Easter morning. The tree of life no longer has to be protected from humans who are on their way to God. Jesus has overcome the distance. The fulfillment of new creation still lies in the future, but we are somehow able to access—and even live into—that future now. N. T. Wright explained this quite succinctly when he said God has done for Jesus in the middle of history what God will do for all of creation at the end of history. Today you will be with me in paradise.

The early church and the Orthodox Church consistently stress the theme that Jesus has defeated death, even tricked death, by entering into it. Every year at the celebration of Easter, the celebrant in the Orthodox Church reads the famous Paschal sermon of St. John Chrysostom, which includes this fabulous line: "[Hell] took a body, and met God face to face. It took earth, and encountered Heaven." The entire sermon is an invitation to all to come and feast at the Table of Life, made open to us by the risen Lord. Chrysostom preaches, "Enjoy ye all the feast of faith: Receive ye all the riches of loving-kindness. Let no one bewail his poverty, for the universal kingdom has been revealed. Let no one weep for his iniquities, for pardon has shown forth from the grave. Let no one fear death, for the Savior's death has set us free. . . . Christ is risen, and life reigns. Christ is risen, and not one dead remains in the grave."

The cross is not the end, and it ends not with forgiveness but with life. In Jesus, God confronts death and enters into it, and then God turns even death into life eternal. My favorite theologian, Jürgen Moltmann, was asked by my friend Travis one time, "Who goes to hell?" Moltmann answered immediately, "Christ."[2] What a beautiful and unexpected answer for those of us who have become so stuck in an individual view of sin and salvation that we have forgotten the unimaginable beauty of a savior who descends even to the depths of hell to bring life to us. There's an ancient liturgy for Holy Saturday that proclaims,

God has died in the flesh, and the underworld has trembled. Truly he goes to seek out our first parent like a lost sheep; he wishes to visit those who sit in darkness and in the shadow of death. He goes to free the prisoner Adam and his fellow-prisoner Eve from their pains, he who is God, and Adam's son . . .

"I am your God, who for your sake became your son, who

2. The Work of the People video, 2015. www.theworkofthepeople.com.

for you and your descendants now speak and command with authority those in prison: Come forth, and those in darkness: Have light, and those who sleep: Rise . . .

"I will reinstate you, no longer in paradise, but on the throne of heaven. I denied you the tree of life, which was a figure, but now I myself am united to you, I who am life."[3]

One of my favorite pieces of Christian art describes this very scene of Jesus descending into hell, and pulling up both Adam and Eve by his hands, setting them in the garden of new life. It's the version of Jesus and the life of the gospel the early church fell in love with, and it's the one that most broadly describes the cosmic power of God's life over all things. From the first humans to the last, Jesus holds us in the grip of life. He is the Great Physician who restores us to wholeness, and the Life of the World, and our joy everlasting. He is our paradise.

3. http://www.vatican.va/spirit/documents/spirit_20010414_omelia-sabato-santo_en.html.

Why the Cross is a Blessing

Up to now, we've talked about the biblical ethic of pursuing life in God, which has meant resting in blessing and following God's commandments and ways. God wants us to grow up and mature, to become aware of good and evil, to choose freely and hopefully wisely, so that we may live faithful lives. And it is absolutely true that God has designed us to live into this calling and has created the world to respond as well. But our experience in the world also tells us we can dutifully till the soil and watch our crops be decimated by a drought. We can eat all our fruits and vegetables and exercise regularly and get cancer. We can work tirelessly to repair a relationship only to watch it fall apart. The reality is, faithfulness cannot be accessed like a vending machine. We can't just put in coins of good effort, twist the dial, and see righteousness gumballs come tumbling into our hands.

It's disappointing and unnerving, because most of us would much rather live in a world ruled by "if, then" clauses. If you follow God, then no harm will come to your loved ones. If you follow God, then you will never doubt. If you follow God, then you won't fall on hard times. But it doesn't work out like that. The world is not a vending machine, but a web. And in the matrix of billions of interconnected actions, spanning years before us and reaching years beyond us, we simply cannot naïvely believe that A is going to reach B in a straight line every time. It's just not that simple.

Nobody had to learn this lesson more painfully than the disciples of Jesus, who watched as the Son of God was led up a hill to die on a cross. If there was ever a human who put in every good righteousness coin there is, it was Jesus. He followed the ways of God without fail. He lived in the life of God and brought it to bear on those around him. He loved perfectly, even after betrayals and abandonments, even after being spit upon and beaten and mocked in the public square. If anyone was guaranteed a good and successful life as an outgrowth of his own actions and intentions, it was Jesus.

Instead, he died a violent, appalling, unfathomable death, not only as a holy man, but as Holy God. In a world where we think we get what we deserve, the most deserving of us all got sold out, abandoned, denied, mocked, beaten, bloodied, and crucified. The cross is the symbol of a cosmic "should not." It is the ferocious antidote of "if, then" faith. Choose life, says Moses. He didn't mention if you do it perfectly, it would get you killed.

You've probably heard it preached before that Jesus' death was scandalous to every conception people had of God in the ancient world. Gods didn't die; they killed people. They didn't show weakness; they imposed their strength with reckless and chaotic abandon. The idea that King Jesus would ride a donkey rather than a chariot into the city as his "triumphal entry" was preposterous. The idea that a god would *die?* Impossible. The cross upended every religious sensibility about what it means to be God.

But it also upended every religious sensibility about what it means to be a faithful follower of God. By every count, Jesus should have been endowed with riches and success and favor and the good life and respect and honor. He should have been living as king in a land overflowing with milk and honey. He should have been the man of the hour, not the man of sorrows acquainted with grief. How did the most faithful human become god-forsaken and crucified? We have nodded our heads as God has showed us again and again that blessing is not if-then but as-is, but we have refused to listen. We want our blessing to be a sign of approval more than we want it to be a sign of unconditional love. More than that, we want a guarantee. We want control. We want to be able to know what to expect out of life, and how to maneuver things to our own benefit.

But this is not God's world. To use biblical language, it's the world of principalities and powers, of the rulers of the age. It's the world of dictators and empires and totalitarian regimes. It's the world of greed and quid pro quo and three strikes you're out. It is a world entirely devoid of blessing. We think we want control, we think we want A-to-B and if-then. We do not realize how gracious God is to refuse our request. We want to be gods, but the painful truth is, we would not rule with grace and blessing like God does. We would rule with iron fists and long lists of compliance. We would demand righteousness and rebuke those who didn't make the cut. We would seek not life but order, not love but control. We would walk around with our self-righteous heads held high, knowing we would *never* allow a world where a righteous man who played by all the rules would get crucified. We would walk around believing we would know the Messiah if we saw him, and fall right in line with everything he asked of us. Ours would be a world of self-imposed virtue and self-sustaining holiness, with no room for weakness or failure or, God forbid, outsiders.

Imagine our surprise when Jesus forgives us our attempts to create this very world in the very act of his dying to it. Imagine our surprise when he dies at the hands of these very powers. Imagine our surprise when he becomes the very things we most want to reject and suppress: weak, vulnerable, abandoned, alone. The message of the cross is foolishness to us when we are perishing, stuck as we are in a demanding world of our own making. But when we see our prison for what it is, when we become those who are being saved, the message of the cross is the power of God. It is the power that blesses and does not curse, the power that gives life and does not bring death. It is divine power freely given to us in a world where we hoard power with anxious fists. It is the power that saves us, not just from sin, but from ourselves.

The cross obliterates the idea of the straight line. You could say it exes it out completely. It spits in the face of proverbs. It mocks any sense of religious propriety. It destabilizes everything we thought we knew about God, and everything we thought we knew about the rewards of following God.

Which is what led J. Louis Martyn to say, "The crucifixion of Jesus Christ is itself the apocalypse."

The word "apocalypse" means to uncover or to reveal. What the cross reveals to us is that we thought we understood what righteousness was, only to realize it was merit instead. We thought we were resting in blessing, when instead we were busy creating structures to justify ourselves. We thought we knew the difference between good and evil, only to find out we were wrong. We thought our eyes had been opened in the garden, as we moved from adolescence to adulthood, only to realize that opening our eyes is a continual exercise, a perpetual vigilance. We first open our eyes as we leave the comforts of the garden, but some eye-opening can only happen in the fertile fields of human choices and worldly realities.

The cross is our invitation to a second coming-of-age, where we are forced once again to rest only in the blessing of God. We have nowhere else to go, once we realize our self-righteousness is less fact and more propaganda. Only the arms of a loving God will do.

Paul sees this truth plainly when he writes in Romans 7:10 the chilling words, "The very commandment that promised life proved to be death to me." What is so shocking, so destabilizing to Paul, is that the very thing that was supposed to bring him life—faithful observance of the Law—brought him death instead. And he's clear to say it isn't the Law's fault, but his. The Law did its job, pointing him toward places where he needed to turn back to God. But the Law isn't a foolproof system, because it only works when our eyes are open, or at least willing to become open. The Law is of no help when we are under the false impression that we have our acts together. This is the most terrifying thing of all, that we can seek the good in religion and still walk straight to our death. We can check all the boxes and still be found wanting. We devise systems to encourage faithfulness only to realize they have trapped us in complacency and ignorance. Who will rescue us from this body of death?!

Just recently, I saw a video clip on the news of a woman who was being interviewed outside a political rally. She said, while looking straight into the camera, "I don't have a racist bone in my body," and then she followed that declaration with one of the most appallingly racist things I had heard in some time. The sad reality is this woman probably doesn't think she has a racist bone in her body. She doesn't see it even as she disparages the human dignity of an entire group of people before a live television camera. And don't think it's just her. It's you and me, too. We may be aware of a good number of our own faults, but we can be sure another handful of them are prancing around dressed like virtues in our minds.

The cross of Christ invades our lives, upends our sensibilities, confounds our senses. It is the armageddon to our constructed desires for virtue and success, not to mention our shallow and self-aggrandizing definitions of blessing itself. The cross is an apocalypse, an unveiling, a terrifying eye-opening, an overturning, a radical revelation about who God is and how God works. We have tried in vain to solve the problem of the cross, as if it's an algebra equation where we need only solve for X. But the biggest problem of the cross is that it is an open question. How can God die? How can the most righteous and perfect human die? It is an unsolvable question, because God means for it to be. More than anything, I believe God intended the cross to be a destabilizing force. It unnerves us as much as it moves us. There's something about the tension of living in-between, of eschewing easy answers, of having to recognize the "but" that refutes all of our assured "if, thens," that forms us into faithful people. There's something about the cross that calls us to open our eyes to the radical notion that all of life is blessing, and we should once and for all put away our report cards, righteousness charts, and faithfulness exams. We have all failed, not only because we have sinned, but because we have thought it wise to keep tabs at all. The cross is God's righteous invasion of blessing in our constructed world of comeuppance.

Martyn writes,

> In the literal crucifixion of Jesus of Nazareth, God invades without a single if. Not if you repent. Not if you learn. Not even if you believe. The absence of the little word if, the uncontingent, prevenient, invading nature of God's grace shows God to be the powerful and victorious Advocate who is intent on the liberation of the entire race of human beings.[1]

We have eschewed original blessing and sought to create a world where we live as righteous inspectors, separating good from evil, only to find that God's own son has not passed

1. J. Louis Martyn, *Theological Issues in the Letters of Paul* (Nashville: Abingdon, 1997), 289.

our own inspection because he simply refused to play by our petty rules. Instead, he has returned us graciously back to the very heart of God, where we are not loved because-of but as-is. God created us and loves us without a single if. And when we have gone and made a mess of things, trying to earn our blessing and prove our worth, God invades our self-righteousness and our blind ignorance without a single if. God invades in the most preposterous, ludicrous, and appalling way possible, by dying at the hands of our systems of righteousness and our empires of worldly justice. In Jesus, God dies to our rejection of blessing.

Meister Eckhart once prayed, "God rid me of God." He wisely understood that his own conception of God, even his own devotion to God, can be the very thing preventing him from faithfulness. In the cross, God answers this prayer, ridding us of the god of virtue, the god of success, the god of just deserts, the god of if-then holiness, until all that is left, all that can be left, is blessing.

In original blessing, we are loved as-is, before we could do anything at all. In the surprising blessing of the cross, we are loved as-is, even after we have done everything imaginable. Even after we have crucified God by our own human hands.

For this reason, Paul contrasts sin in Romans 5 not to forgiveness, not even to life, but to the free gift from God. Out of nowhere, from one verse to the next, Paul changes his wording, emphasizing the distinction of the free gift of grace once, twice, three times, in contrast to the condemnation of sin. Paul tells us where sin abounds, grace abounds all the more. Scholars say the word here in Greek is more aptly described as super-abounds. It's a radical and abundant contrast between the power of sin, destructive as it is to keep us ensnared even when we don't know it, and the power of grace made known to us in Jesus, which leads us finally and completely to nothing short of everlasting, abundant life in God.

In Jesus, we realize to our great delight and to our unending surprise that even our participation in death itself, and death of God no less, cannot separate us from our blessing. We can choose a path so terrifying that we end up crucifying the Son of God, and God will turn our evil into an empty tomb on Easter morning. We can take the One who is the Bread of Life, the One who is the Living Water, the One who is the Light of the World, and we can drive nails through his hands and his feet and watch him die on a hill in the public square, and God will look upon our horrifying actions and lead us to yet another garden, with yet another man and woman, where we find the risen Jesus, who sees Mary Magdalene not hiding in the bushes but searching for her savior. Jesus says, "Woman, why are you weeping? Whom are you looking for?" Mary thinks he is the gardener, because she cannot see him with those pre-Easter eyes, and she begs him, "Sir, if you have carried him away, tell me where you have laid him." And then Jesus says her name—"Mary!"—and her eyes are opened.

And so we return to the most important thing any of us need to know:

> But now thus says the Lord,
>   he who created you,
>   he who formed you:
> Do not fear, for I have redeemed you;
>   I have called you by name, you are mine.

We belong to God. We always have, and we always will. God has called us by name, and we are God's.

We have belonged to God since our first breath, since our earliest years in the garden of God's family. But much has happened since we left home. We have found ourselves in a world of joy and a world of horror. We have found, to our great despair, that we are not only aware of evil but capable of it. We are capable of killing even the Son of God, and we are numb at the realization. In the swirling storm of good and evil, we so easily lose our blessing. So Jesus brings us back to a garden, but it is a garden teeming with the kind of life that comes only at the cost of a world-shattering, paradigm-questioning death. We enter that garden confused and disoriented, but wanting desperately to find God, only to realize with utter desperation that we can see nothing at all. We cannot see Jesus until he calls us by name.

And so he does. He calls us, as he called Mary, as he would call the disciples, even Thomas, who doubted him, and Peter, who denied him. He calls the travelers on the road to Emmaus, whose eyes are opened when Jesus breaks bread with them. And at the end, Jesus takes his disciples out as far as Bethany, and he lifts up his hands, and he blesses them. Luke then ends his gospel with these words: *They were continually in the temple, blessing God.* In Jesus, with Jesus, through Jesus, blessing has come full circle.

Blessing comes before us, and blessing comes beside us, and blessing goes ahead of us to the ends of the earth. God gives us original blessing, but that is not all. God gives us the blessing of new life, of new creation, of clean slates and grace that is new every morning. So we find ourselves returning to the word-prayer *dayenu*, where we tell God one gift would have been enough, but God has gone again and given far more than that. It would have been enough if God alone had called us by name, but Jesus is God's Dayenu, who calls our name not from the far reaches of heaven but from the pits of our own human hell. Jesus calls us, and sets our feet in the garden of life once again. I would say Jesus is God's final Dayenu, but that wouldn't be true. Jesus sends us the Spirit, who not only calls us by name but prays and even groans on our behalf, eclipsing the distance between our feelings of despair and the presence of God's peace. God's blessing is abundant, and God's grace has no end.

Paul tells us, since we are justified by faith, we have peace with God, because God's love has been poured into our hearts through the Holy Spirit that has been given to us. It would have been enough that God's love has been poured out to us in the act of creation. It would have been enough that Jesus' love has been poured out for us in the act of crucifixion and resurrection. It would have been enough that the Spirit's love has been poured into our hearts. But God is a God of abundance, not a God of enough. And so God keeps giving, over and over again. Because of this, we can say with Paul that our hope in God does not disappoint us. Our hope in God does not promise us ease or even worldly stability. Our hope in God does not remove us from a world acquainted with both joy and sorrow. But our hope in God does not disappoint us, because God's love is the steadiest thing the cosmos has to offer. We can rest in God's steadfast faithfulness even after we have crucified the Son of God. What an unfathomable mystery. Once we realize that's true, we can begin to know the depths of the deepest truth of all: nothing can separate us from the love of God in Christ Jesus. Nothing.

God's love is not contingent on ifs. It is a free gift of grace. It is a blessing. It began as a blessing, it became human and dwelt among us as blessing, it will end in blessing. So here is the beautiful revelation in the blessing of Jesus. Our lives are not only sustained by the golden thread of original blessing. (Dayenu.) Our lives are also entirely sustained by the resurrected life of the crucified Christ. We can say, with all hope and with all conviction, that the grace of our Lord Jesus Christ, and the love of God, and the fellowship of the Holy Spirit, will be with us all, now and forever.

May all God's children, every last one of God's children, say Amen.

So, Why Jesus?

From Genesis to Revelation, God continually calls us to life. We are called to be people of life in a world of both life and death. And certainly, we see these tensions at the heart of the

New Testament story. Jesus employs imagery teeming with life—vine and branches, bread and wine, water and mustard seeds.

And yet, I'm so haunted by the response I got from that Catholic priest in the elevator, only because I'm fairly certain it's a widespread and common point of view. If we don't have a sin nature, then why do we need Jesus?

God has sent us into the fertile land and given us the formidable task of wrenching life from the hardened soil and our very bodies, and we daily face the tensions of living between harmony and disharmony, re-creation and degradation, glory and ruin. We live in the shadow of the constant tension of good and evil, and of life and death, and we are only halfway to wisdom if we're being honest. And that's on a good day.

So we need help. God help us, we pray. We need help. We need some guidance, and a helping hand, and some concrete examples, because life out here east of Eden can feel like we have entirely lost our way.

So God has sent God's only son, full of grace and truth. He came to remind us of what we needed to know most, which is that this God is sticking with it even when we've long thrown in the towel. He comes to bear this most precious name, Emmanuel. Jesus comes to us, not to fix us, but to save us. He comes so that the message of God-with-us is made real in the flesh and blood of human experience and the wind and sun of life on earth.

Jesus comes, born into the complicated world of a Roman census and no room in the inn and pagan astrologers and the massacre of the holy innocents. So we know he understands. He understands when we say we experience nothing but endless cycles of stabilization and destabilization, because this is the world he lived in, and the world he came to save. And he begins to save it almost immediately, because those pagan astrologers lay gifts at his feet and call him King in a world of violent dictators and competing foreign allegiances. He begins to save it because even old Simeon who can't see five feet in front of him can feel a rumbling in his heart and an echo deep down in his bones when baby Jesus arrives in the Temple, like a light straight from God and a big sigh of relief from the heavens as if to say, "I keep my promises." He saves it because he grows in wisdom and in stature, and in favor with God and all the rest of us, stabilizing most everyone around him, until he embarks on his own rebellious journey away from his parents so he can stand in the Temple and declare, "Today this prophecy has been fulfilled in your hearing" and sit back down like he said nothing remarkable at all, destabilizing everything we think we knew about God. He saves it by walking down to the Jordan and being covered by the waters of baptism and he saves it by walking in Galilee and healing all who came to his door and he saves by seeing all the people our sin-sick eyes had forgotten and all the people our holy sunglasses wouldn't allow and he blesses them, over and over he blesses them, while he takes the lunch of a small boy and feeds us all with it, because he is nothing short of life abundant. He saves us because every parable he tells and every story he preaches comforts the afflicted and afflicts the comforted and leaves us all both questioning what we thought and wondering what to do, because that's what happens when truth hits you, and that's how wisdom is cultivated, right in the heart of the rocks and thistles of what we thought was settled soil.

Jesus saves us because he turns his face toward Jerusalem when two thousand years later we still turn our faces away, and he weeps over the city and walks toward it still. He saves us because he feeds us all at his table, even the one who betrayed him, which is to say, all of us. Because we all have cherished a bag of silver coins over the life of our Savior, and we have done so when far less was at stake. Jesus saves us because he tells Peter to put his sword away and he heals that soldier right there in the middle of yet another garden, because he is the tree of life no matter where he is standing. He saves us because he is God even when he is crucified and he blesses us even as we curse him and send him to die. He saves us because he enters the hell of betrayal and God-forsakenness so that we know there is no place we cannot go where he is not with us.

And that is why he came. Not to fix our sin problem but to fix our blessing problem, which is that we are in the terrifying and tragic habit of forgetting we have one, and that it comes from a God who will do anything and everything to be with us.

God has been trying to tell us this all along.

We need Jesus because in him there is no darkness at all, and in him the fullness and wisdom of God was pleased to dwell. In him we become what God the Father has intended for us to become all along: brothers and sisters, children of God, who reside in a land teeming with blessing.

Why do we need Jesus? Because we need to remember, more than anything else, that we are in a relationship with God, and God started it, and God has promised to finish it with nothing short of abundant life. God has given us beauty for ashes, strength for anguish, gladness for mourning, and peace for despair. And in Jesus, God has returned even death itself for life abundant, even violence into peace, even the depths of the terrors of the human heart into a triumph of faithfulness and redemption.

We need Jesus because we are children of God who no longer live at home in the garden, and we need our Brother to help us find our way back home.

V. Living into Blessing

Practice, Not Perfect

The goodness God gives us in original blessing, we remember, is both an origin and a goal. It is our anchor, and it is also our calling. Blessing is, and blessing becomes. How do we live into our blessing? In a word, practice. We do it by practicing our faith, every day. I'm strongly in favor of using the word "practice" because it takes the pressure off. We are not playing in the World Championships or the Olympics every day. We are here to give it a try—to give it our best try, when we're able—but if we mess up, we do not have to crumple down to the ground or berate ourselves. In the next hour, in the next minute, we will have another chance to practice again. When our goal is an integrated life of faith, everything counts as practice. Every moment can be an opportunity to become more loving, more aware, more just, more gracious, more forgiving, less judgmental, less anxious, more at peace.

When we see faith as practice, we also let go of the need to know exactly what we're doing. We probably don't, and that's fine. (Or we think we do when we don't!) When we practice, we will pick it up as we go. We may not really understand prayer until we spend hours doing it. We may return to a scripture story again and again and see different things each time. We may decide to start practicing justice in our daily routines only to forget about it for weeks. While we seek to follow God faithfully, we can do so with grace. It's not the ivy leagues. It's practice.

We shouldn't underestimate how vital our practice is, though. To be a disciple is to be an apprentice to the ways of God. We work and we build and we study and we learn by example and we learn from mistakes and we keep showing up. We do this not out of some need to be accepted or some desire to prove ourselves but because we find value in creating a life of meaning and purpose, of aligning our lives with life in God. We do it to inhabit abundant life. Of all the ways we could choose to be in the world, we have decided to be people who live according to the ways of God and the example of Jesus. We want to make beautiful things, not least of them being our own lives.

Our practices and habits and structures are the way we live out what we value and what we desire. If we are consistent in forming life-giving rhythms, we will find before long that we do them without even thinking. Of course, that's true also for those habits and practices that keep us in patterns of unfaithfulness. What we do, knowingly or unknowingly, determines who we become.

What we do and become is of course greatly affected by other influences, people and patterns all around us. The idea that we have individual personalities we came up with all on our own is patently untrue. We are far more than just nature or nurture. We are a nexus of receptors, constantly interpreting, reacting, and patterning ourselves after all that happens around us. Anthropologist Pierre Bourdieu coined the word *habitus* to describe this interconnected system of our practices and actions, which contains both the complexities of our individual patterns and the patterns we make as groups, a society, and as a whole. A habitus includes "lasting dispositions, trained capacities and structured propensities to think, feel and act in determinant ways."[1] In other words, in an interconnected society, we are constantly choosing and being influenced to choose certain practices, and those practices fashion not only what we do but how we think and feel. We create habits, and habits create us.

Instead of saying practice makes perfect, then, we can say practice makes pathways. It can create pathways that lead us to life, or pathways that lead us away from it. But when we practice, the neurons firing in our brain make pathways, and the muscle memory in our body makes pathways, and the habits of our daily rituals make pathways. Whatever we do, whether in word or deed, we can do as a pathway to the name of God.

A number of years ago, I began to feel that I needed more silent prayer in my life. I spend my days talking about God, thinking about God, teaching and writing about God, and I sensed I needed to balance out all that jibber-jabber with the simple act of being with God, with nothing on the agenda. So I began to pray silently. At first, the impulse to fill that

1. Z. Navarro, "In Search of Cultural Interpretation of Power," *IDS Bulletin* 37, no. 6 (2006): 11–22.

silence with words was nearly unbearable. When my mouth wasn't talking, my mind was going ninety miles an hour. But I found that with practice, little by little, I began to get comfortable with the silence. And eventually, I began to crave it. Being silently with God remains one of the most rejuvenating spiritual practices in my life. But if you had told me that five years ago, I would hardly have believed it.

That's true for communities of faith, too. I've found there's nothing more awkward than asking young people to be silent in group settings. We are so used to the constant noise of our phones and the podcast or music playing in our earbuds and the relentless hum of our world, we've lost much of our capacity to be still in silence. My community of faith decided to begin our gathering with a few moments of silence before we prayed the collect together. We would stand, and breathe, just long enough to take note of the breath in our lungs and the gravity pulling at our feet, just long enough to push into awkward silence until it became a little more bearable. And do you know what? We realized we loved it, and needed it, and felt more focused in the gathering because of it. Practice makes pathways. We are formed and shaped by what we do.

As we grow and mature in faith, we seek to become more aware of our habits, if not the entire habitus in which we exist, instead of allowing them to run unconsciously in the background. By becoming aware, and by living with intention, we become active agents in our own lives and in the world.

Work It Out/God Works in You

Perhaps the best example of the agency we're given in blessing is Philippians 2:12–13. "Work out your own salvation with fear and trembling; for it is God who is at work in you, enabling you both to will and to work for God's good pleasure." We realize our blessing calls us to live faithfully, which means it is our responsibility to act and practice our discipleship in the way of God, while in the same breath we remember God is at work within us, equipping us with every good gift for this work. We live in the dynamic fusion of divine and human agency.

Holding these realities in tension prevents us from seeing our actions as autonomous, which goes against our understanding of blessing and our place in a relationally interconnected world. But it also prevents us from seeing our faith as total dependence on God in a way that takes away our sense of responsibility and human agency. God doesn't want us to be autonomous or dependent. God wants us to be relationally connected in a healthy and life-giving way to God, to others, and to all of creation. God gives us agency to live and work in the world as God's people to cultivate generative relationships in all we do. God wants us to live with intention while nested in blessing.

Paul describes this same agency in Romans 6 when he mentions something very interesting, something that hints all the way back to Genesis 4. He says, "Therefore, do not let sin exercise dominion in your mortal bodies." Sin crouches at our door, just like always, but Paul's words remind us of the very thing God told Cain: *timshel.* You must master it. And in Jesus, you may master it. For Paul, it's so obvious, it's a command. Don't let sin exercise dominion. And then he goes on to say, don't present yourselves as instruments of wickedness, but as instruments of righteousness.

The Greek word Paul uses for instruments, *melos,* is the same word he uses in Romans 12 when he's talking about our different functions as members of Christ's body, and the same word he uses in 1 Corinthians 6 when he asks, "Do you not know that you are members of Christ's body?" While in the New Testament letters *melos* is most often translated as members, the Greeks used *melos* to describe both weapons of war and parts of a ship. It's the idea of being part of a larger whole. Sometimes, those parts come together for destruction, and other times they come together to form a ship that can ride the waves of the sea. What we do as our part affects the entire system. We're all connected. We can act as weapons, or we can act as instruments.

We can act as weapons, or we can turn our weapons into plowshares and pruning hooks. This well-known imagery from the Old Testament is usually quoted in Isaiah 2, but it actually occurs in Micah 4 and in Joel 3 as well. It's no wonder, as the imagery of beating a sword into a gardening tool is a powerful description of the life of faith, where we take what is destructive and turn it into something that brings life. This is what it looks like to participate in the life of God.

A friend of mine once sent me a photograph of a tree sculpture made entirely out of assault weapons. I remember being struck at the sheer volume of guns that were needed to make the tree, and feeling a little heartsick at the idea of forced child soldiers in Uganda who were required to carry them, and worse, use them. But I also remember being moved by the silhouette of this black iron tree, defiantly projecting a symbol of life even out of weapons that had caused such harm. Redemption is something we experience as a gift from God, and it's also something we do when the spirit of God moves us. God makes dead things alive, and though that's not literally possible for us, art, poetry, music, and story are ways we too participate in bringing new life to dead things.

An Expanding Agency

Much like our blessing expands from Genesis to the Gospels and beyond, we can see our agency expand as the story of God continues. The blessing began in the garden, but it continues in the people who carry God's blessing forward as agents of faithfulness.

When God calls Abraham, God reveals that in him, all the nations of the earth will be blessed. From the beginning, blessing was never something to be hoarded, but to be shared. Blessing by its very nature generates life. Blessing is not a trophy on a shelf but a light to guide us in all we do. We are blessed to be a blessing. We are blessed to enrich every one of our connections with the light of God's steadfast love.

Moses called the Israelites to a life of faithful agency, too. When he gave his "Choose life or death" speech in

Deuteronomy 30, the last section of his call to action is a declaration of human agency.

> Surely, this commandment that I am commanding you today is not too hard for you, nor is it too far away. It is not in heaven, that you should say, "Who will go up to heaven for us, and get it for us so that we may hear it and observe it?" Neither is it beyond the sea, that you should say, "Who will cross to the other side of the sea for us, and get it for us so that we may hear it and observe it?" No, the word is very near to you; it is in your mouth and in your heart for you to observe.

The word has always been near to us, because following God is not foreign to us but the way God has designed for us to live.

In Jesus, God has brought the word even closer to us. The Word made flesh has now entered our human experience. Jesus has shown us the way to live abundantly in God, and has anchored his own blessing and word in our hearts, that we may do it. We find it difficult enough to believe that Jesus equips us to live faithfully, but Jesus himself proclaimed something even more radical in John 14:12 when he said, "Very truly, I tell you, the one who believes in me will also do the works that I do and, in fact, will do greater works than these." Jesus doesn't want us to stay in his shadow. He wants us to participate in his life.

Through the gift of the Holy Spirit, we are given even more agency to live as God calls us. The Spirit guides us into all truth, which is not a knowing but an abiding. The Spirit is our Advocate, who Jesus says will teach us everything, and remind us of all that he has said to us.[2] And we know that where the Spirit is, there is freedom. We are free to live as agents of grace, peace, justice, and love. We can find joy in walking in the ways of God. We can, as Jesus told the man at the end of the parable of the good Samaritan, go and do likewise.

Prayer: The Practice of Clarity

Practice makes pathways. And one of the most essential pathways as we seek to become people who live with intention while resting in blessing, is prayer.

Prayer connects us to our golden thread of blessing. When we pray, we attune ourselves to the presence of God. We don't have to do anything or say anything, even. Sitting quietly before God and recognizing the blessed "enough" of God's presence is all we need. Because we live in a world so often filled with messages that counteract our sense of blessing, it's good practice to remove ourselves from the noise and settle into the resonant hum of our Beloved.

The more we live into a rhythm of praying and sensing the presence of God, the more we become familiar with the feeling of God's presence. The more familiar we are, the more skilled we will be in finding it when we realize we have lost connection to our sense of blessing. On those days when we fall off our faith bikes, we can allow blessing to cover our scrapes and bruises like holy aloe, soothing us and reminding us we are loved as-is, and we can get back up and start pedaling again.

2. John 14:26.

The great gift of prayer is that we can do it anywhere, even if just for a moment. We can close our eyes in the middle of a conflict or rush-hour traffic or the cries of a screaming baby or the tension of a high-stakes board meeting and know that God is there waiting for us. God is with us. We need not ask, or plead. God is here, among us, and God's blessing has been with us here all the time.

As we seek to live into the beautiful fusion of divine and human agency that is our life on earth, we find clarity and centeredness when we take time to pray. As we pray, the way becomes known to us, maybe not in details or concrete steps, but in an intuitive sense of how to be, even if we don't yet know what to do. Prayer invites us to stop, breathe, collect ourselves, sense that God is here, among us, within us. In prayer, we search for that anchored place of blessing, that golden thread residing at the center of our being, guiding us onwards and forwards into abundant life. In prayer, we hear the song God sings over each and every one of us, calling us to harmony and inviting us to live as instruments of blessing.

Serpents, Doves, and Eyeglasses

What saves a man is to take a step. Then another step. It is always the same step, but you have to take it.

—Antoine de Saint-Exupéry

Rocky Byun is a balancing expert. He travels around South Korea and the world, stacking motorcycles on rocks and laptops on coffee cups. When you see his work, it's hard not to believe it's an illusion. How does he get a chair—with a person in it—to balance on one leg?! Byun, who has studied physics, says he simply finds the center of gravity in each object. And sure, he knows a lot about physics to understand what to look for and how to manipulate the objects to shift their balance. But a skill like that is never only equations, but also a deep, embodied kind of knowing. Rocky Byun knows what balance feels like, and he can search for it and find it in eggs and traffic cones and the kickstand of a bicycle because he knows it is already waiting there for him.

Every object in the universe has a center of gravity. Ours is original blessing. Original blessing grounds us in the steadfast, unwavering, unbreakable love of God even when our world feels as if it might topple over any moment. We find in God our center of gravitas, our essential dignity, our deepest worth. We are children of God, and we are beloved.

We begin with blessing, and as we go along, we realize blessing is also our companion, and our end. The bonds we feel with God, others, and even ourselves will ebb and flow, which is natural. By remembering our blessing, we give ourselves permission to move with grace and freedom and not get caught up in the exhausting pursuit of perfection or even consistency. And we are released from the unbearable weight of shame, which is such a relief.

Wise as Serpents, Innocent as Doves

As we think about what it means to live into blessing, I'm reminded of Jesus' admonition to his disciples to be wise as serpents and innocent as doves. We're not used to hearing serpents called wise, especially as we've so demonized them (pun intended) in our readings of Genesis and elsewhere. But Jesus shows in his words an acceptance that we carry with us the very fruit of the garden: we hold within us the knowledge of both good and evil. As we go forth as his disciples, our calling is not to banish the knowledge of evil, but to funnel it toward our pursuit of wisdom. Be wise as serpents, Jesus said. In a world where there indeed is sin and separation from God and one another, only wisdom will do.

Be wise as a serpent when evil and sin crouch at your doorstep. Be wise as a serpent when vengeance or violence try to take root in your heart. Be wise as a serpent when systems of injustice threaten to catch us in their web. Be wise as a serpent when your yetzer hara/drive wants to run the show. Be wise as a serpent when someone is trying to take advantage of you, and all you can see is destruction in their eyes. Be wise as a serpent, which carries within it both the poison that kills and the poison that heals. Only the wise know how much to use, and when, to find healing.

And also, be innocent as doves. Keep your heart as light as a feather and your wings poised for flight, homing in on your center of gravity that is with you wherever you go. Be innocent as doves and little children, whose eyes behold the wonder of the world without need of explanation. Be innocent as doves, who look upon people with love and trust and even expectation. Be innocent as doves, who do not sow or reap or hoard things in barns, but walk through life with fists unclenched and arms outstretched. Be innocent as doves by living as those who dare to believe that blessing is true in the face of those who would rather you forget it.

Be wise as serpents by being aware of our human potential to do wrong. Be innocent as doves by encouraging our human potential to do good.

Like Rocky Byun, who balances glass pitchers on top of green apples, find your way into the movement that is both yetzer hara/drive and yetzer hatov/conscience, the knowledge of both good and evil, the acceptance of both life and death. When you miss the mark, as surely you will, see it as an opportunity to know your faults more clearly, to become aware of something you may have needed to know, and allow that new wisdom to draw you closer to God and others. Sin can separate, but it can also turn us around. Archbishop Desmond Tutu says perfect love is not reactive but responsive. The same is true for blessing. Wherever we find ourselves, whatever we are doing, we can respond to blessing, to love, and find life on the other side. We do not have to react. We have room inside us to be both wise and innocent.

Love Calls Us Home

Jürgen Moltmann once said, "We are not loved because we are beautiful and good. We are beautiful and good because we are loved."[1] Original sin, because it puts us on the defensive, often forces us to seek love because we fear we don't have it. We try to earn God's love. Or, we try to debase ourselves because we think that's what God wants. We become eager workers or resigned pessimists. In blessing, we remember instead what Moltmann so elegantly stated. We are given the ability to walk with God because we are loved, but God's love never rests on our walking. We remember that original blessing grounds us and the blessing of Jesus envelops us, so that there is love in every direction.

You are loved when you get that job and you are loved when you don't. You are loved when your marriage fails, you are loved when you celebrate your sixtieth wedding anniversary, and you are loved when you never get married at all, and never want to. You are loved when you rank first

---

1. Yale Divinity School, "Theology of Joy: Jürgen Moltmann & Miroslav Volf." *YouTube*. 14 Aug. 2014. Web. 28 Apr. 2016.

in your marathon and you are loved when you rank highest in your cancer cell count. You are loved. When everything else in reality is in flux, whether it's the prosperity of the mountain or the tragedy of the valley, God's love is still there. It is unwavering. Every object in the universe has a center of gravity, and yours, dear blessed child of God, is the ever-faithful love of God.

When You Lose Your Way: A Benediction

I'm supposed to wear glasses, but since I don't like them, I rarely do. What this means is that I'm normally a little fuzzy in my view of things, and also that I never quite know where my glasses are. (If I ignore you from across the room, it's because I probably can't see you.) I shift them from purse to purse or bag to bag. I leave them on my nightstand. I set them down, for reasons unknown, in my closet. I wish I could say I tend to find them on top of my head, but I hardly ever put them on at all. The other day I was looking for my glasses again, this time because I actually wanted to use them, so I was digging through a list of usual suspect locations. Once I found them, I put them on and realized, as I always do, that being able to see clearly is such a welcome relief. The world looks so much crisper and more vibrant, and I feel like I can see for miles. What a difference! It's mesmerizing! I have no idea why I refuse to wear them on a daily basis.

I don't know where you are with blessing, but I imagine at least some of you may feel about it the way I do about my glasses. You may know it's there, and even keep it near enough to you, but you may not be as consistent at letting it focus your view. That's normal. That's often the way of things. I was talking with an old friend recently about being grounded in original blessing and she said, "Oh, I don't think I'm good at that at all." And then we laughed, because it's such an honest and yet ironic thing to say. We are steeped in a culture that tells us to be good at things or else, and that's sometimes never truer than within the four walls of a church. We're earnest in wanting to be good at blessing, but it's really beside the point. God is fantastic at blessing, so take a deep breath. You're off the hook.

My friend Paul Soupiset is an amazing and talented artist, and he sent me this beautiful print he drew that says, "Just show up." I love it so much, because whenever I'm feeling very Danielle-the-honor-student about things, I can take one look at that and be reminded it's not so complicated. Most of life is just showing up, which, don't get me wrong, is hard enough to do. It's plenty. But when we move into life with a willingness to be present, we're often surprised at the energy of life that meets us there. Blessing isn't one more thing for you to be good at. It's the one place where you don't have to do anything at all but just show up. Are you just sitting there? Good. God is there, with blessing in hand. It's that easy.

And yet, sometimes it feels so very hard. I've sat beside people who are looking for that golden thread of blessing with enough determination to hike Mount Kilimanjaro, and it still feels impossible to grasp. I wish I knew what to say in those moments to fix it immediately, but as with many things, it is a mystery. And as with many things, I probably couldn't fix it if I tried. What I can say is that when I find myself in those moments, I try to remember that God's blessing is not based on feeling it. It's there whether you can see it or not, whether you feel it or not, even whether you can accept it or not. It's always there. And somehow, it will become known to you again. You'll open your eyes from one moment to the next and realize the world is crisp and vibrant again, teeming with life. And alas, the clarity may last only for a moment, but it may be enough to remind you it's been there all along.

Living into our original blessing does not shelter us from difficulty. As I said before, it isn't magic. Blessing does provide a centering place as we make our way *through* difficulty, but it does not prevent it. It may, in all honesty, bring even more difficulty into our path, because blessing requires us to be open to the world in challenging ways. When we acknowledge the deep connectedness of God's creation, we are also open to one another's pain.

We cannot lose our blessing, but it's hard to know what do we do when we feel we have lost our way. When God feels far from us, or we feel we have ruined things, or we are confronted with profound feelings of shame or failure, we don't always know how to find blessing in the midst of that.

One of the primary difficulties we face as humans is anxiety and fear, rooted in inadequacy. This inadequacy can take shape in many forms. When I was writing this book, I had days where I felt ungracious and negative toward others. I would grumble at the slowness of the person in the checkout line, or overreact when one of my children did something. I'd think to myself, "Well, great. I can't write any more today, now that I have totally lost my sense of blessing." What a silly thing to say. If we wait until we get it right or get our acts together, we will never begin at all. And besides, this is precisely why God gives us blessing to begin with. We do not find our grounding in our own actions, but in the love of God. If we place our grounding anywhere else, we will eventually sport the wobbling ankles to prove it.

While it makes sense to lose our grounding during a difficult moment or season, it can often be worse when we find our grounding in our successes. We feel so light, so fulfilled, so proud of ourselves. We think, "I have finally lived into my blessing! It feels wonderful!" only to feel the emptiness that comes when the glories of success dissipate in the coming days or weeks. Pride indeed comes before the fall.

My friend Barbara, who has practiced meditation for years, says this kind of thing happens to her all the time in her practice. She'll be meditating with a flurry of thoughts, and then it will get quiet and her breath will be in sync and she'll think, "Yes! I'm doing great! Now I am really feeling it!" And before she can finish the thought, all the noise comes rushing right back in. Fixating on centeredness often means losing it, ironically enough. We cannot possess centeredness, or own it. When we grab for it, it slips away entirely. We can only inhabit it, because it is too big for us to hold. It is the same with blessing.

So it's wise to be careful not to label achievements as blessing when they are actually just worldly success. Blessing likely inspires and undergirds our success, but we risk the danger of believing we earn our blessedness when we align them too closely. We will know we are centering on true blessedness when we can feel the same acceptance of God on the days we triumph gloriously and on the days we fail miserably.

Blessing is our anchor, our constant. We do not pick up blessing and carry it with us, only to realize we have dropped it and must retrace our steps and find it again. Blessing carries us, and we do not need to struggle to find it. It has not gone anywhere. Blessing is never lost. We only need to stop and reconnect with it. It has been there all the time. Or, more precisely, God has been there all the time. And God does not dole out blessing in stingy portions. The blessing we have is more than enough. It is more than enough, to grow on.

Because God has designed the world relationally, we can find glimpses of our blessing in others, of course, too. When our gremlins begin to growl in our ears, we begin to imagine and assume the voices and opinions of people who dislike us, or at least don't know us very well. Instead, we can remember those who love us best, and turn our ears from the gremlins to our actual friends. They, too, might have difficult words for us to hear, but we will be able to receive them, because we trust that they know us and want what is best for us. Our dearest beloveds love us in spite of ourselves, and in this reflection of God's steady love for us, we, too, can find our way home, even if our pride is a little hurt.

Since we cannot possess blessing, we live into our blessing anew each moment. While you could see that as bad news, imagining you must find your grounding in blessing over and over again, you can also see it as good news of relief.

When we lose our way, here comes a veritable stream of moments in which to find our way back home again. Living into blessing requires us to let go of our own sense of constancy. Humans are too complex and unwieldy for that (made in the image of a God who is *definitely* too complex and unwieldy for that), and such a demand rejects the true nature of the universe, which has always been one of change. Because God is steadfast, we do not have to demand it of ourselves. Blessing does not have requirements, remember. It is a gift.

So take heart: you are not alone when you lose your way. God remains with you, and you are surrounded by every other human who also struggles with feelings of despair, shame, humiliation, depression, and fear. You may have lost your sense of blessing multiple times just in reading these pages, and that is okay. These feelings are to be both expected and accepted. You do not have to be "good at" receiving blessing. You can receive it as poorly as you lost it, and trust that the truth of the blessing itself will transform you nevertheless. Draw close to God in prayer, and dare to believe that you are God's treasured beloved. Because that, dear child of God, is precisely and always what you are.

Acknowledgments

I'm so grateful to Fortress Press for creating Theology for the People, and I'm honored to be in such great company. Thanks to Tony Jones for being enthusiastic about this idea and for always shooting me straight, to Lisa Gruenisen for her skillful (and rapid!) editing prowess, and to the entire Fortress Press team.

I offer deep gratitude to Matthew Fox, who coined the term original blessing in his book of the same name, and who pioneered the resurgence of its theology. I hope by using this term and encouraging others to do so, it might come into more common usage.

I owe a good deal to the many friends who engaged me in countless conversations about blessing and sin over the past couple of years. Thanks for bringing up thoughtful questions, reading bad drafts, and generally being fantastic. I'm particularly indebted to my professor friends, who allowed me to inundate them with questions about early church history, biblical languages, theological minutiae, and other matters on which I'm no expert. Thank you. I do want to say a special thanks to Luke Miller, who should earn an Eagle Scout-level merit badge for his encouragement and consistently helpful feedback.

I dedicate this book to Dan, who daily shows me what love looks like when it is faithful, steadfast, spacious, and freeing. Dan, Mia, and Grant, you are and will always remain my most treasured blessings.

Bibliography

Alison, James. *The Joy of Being Wrong: Original Sin through Easter Eyes.* New York: Crossroad, 1998.

Augustine. *Anti-Pelagian Writings: On Marriage and Concupsicence. Christian Classics Ethereal Library.* http://www.ccel.org/ccel/schaff/npnf105.xvi.v.html.

Augustine, and R. S. Pine-Coffin. *Confessions.* Harmondsworth, Middlesex, England: Penguin, 1961.

Balentine, Samuel E., and Bruce C. Birch. *And God Saw That It Was Good: Essays on Creation and God in Honor of Terence E. Fretheim.* St. Paul: Luther Seminary, 2006. Print. Word & World Theology for Christian Ministry, Supplemental Ser.

Barclay, John M. G., Martinus C. De Boer, Susan Eastman, Neil Elliott, and Beverly Roberts Gaventa. *Apocalyptic Paul.* Waco, TX: Baylor University Press, 2013.

Barclay, John M. G., and Simon J. Gathercole. *Divine and Human Agency in Paul and His Cultural Environment.* London: T. & T. Clark, 2006.

Brock, Rita Nakashima, and Rebecca Ann Parker. *Saving Paradise: How Christianity Traded Love of This World for Crucifixion and Empire.* Boston: Beacon, 2008.

Brueggemann, Walter. *Genesis*. Atlanta: John Knox, 1982.

Capps, Donald. *The Depleted Self: Sin in a Narcissistic Age*. Minneapolis: Fortress Press, 1993.

Charlesworth, James H. *The Good and Evil Serpent: How a Universal Symbol Became Christianized*. New Haven: Yale University Press, 2010.

Eibl-Eibesfeldt, Irenäus. *Love and Hate: The Natural History of Behavior Patterns*. New York: Holt, Rinehart & Winston, 1971.

Ellingsen, Mark. *Blessed Are the Cynical: How Original Sin Can Make America a Better Place*. Grand Rapids: Brazos, 2003.

Girard, René. *I See Satan Fall Like Lightning*. Maryknoll, NY: Orbis, 2001.

Hari, Johann. *Chasing the Scream: The First and Last Days of the War on Drugs*. New York: Bloomsbury, 2015.

Irenaeus. *Irenaeus against Heresies*. Whitefish, MT: Kessinger, 2007.

Jacobs, Alan. *Original Sin: A Cultural History*. New York: HarperOne, 2008.

Johnson, Luke Timothy. *Reading Romans: A Literary and Theological Commentary*. New York: Crossroad, 1997.

Kierkegaard, Søren, Reidar Thomte, and Albert Anderson. *The Concept of Anxiety: A Simple Psychologically Orienting Deliberation on the Dogmatic Issue of Hereditary Sin*. Princeton: Princeton University Press, 1980.

Korsmeyer, Jerry D. *Evolution and Eden: Balancing Original Sin and Contemporary Science*. New York: Paulist, 1998.

Lieber, David L., and Jules Harlow. *Etz Hayim: Torah and Commentary*. Philadelphia: Jewish Publication Society, 2001.

Lossky, Vladimir. *Orthodox Theology: An Introduction*. Crestwood, NY: St. Vladimir's Seminary Press, 1978.

MacIsaac, Sharon. *Freud and Original Sin*. New York: Paulist, 1974.

Martyn, J. Louis. *Theological Issues in the Letters of Paul*. Nashville: Abingdon, 1997.

Meyer, Paul W., and John T. Carroll. *The Word in This World: Essays in New Testament Exegesis and Theology*. Louisville: Westminster John Knox, 2004.

Mesters, Carlos. *Eden, Golden Age or Goad to Action?* Maryknoll, NY: Orbis, 1974.

Metzger, Bruce M., and Michael David Coogan. *The Oxford Companion to the Bible*. New York: Oxford University Press, 1993.

Mitchell, Christopher Wright. *The Meaning of BRK "to Bless" in the Old Testament*. Atlanta: Scholars, 1987.

Moltmann, Jürgen. *God in Creation: A New Theology of Creation and the Spirit of God*. San Francisco: Harper & Row, 1985.

Myers, Benjamin. "A Tale of Two Gardens: Augustine's Narrative Interpretation of Romans 5," in *Apocalyptic Paul: Cosmos and Anthropos in Romans 5-8*. Waco, TX: Baylor University Press, 2013.

Newell, J. Philip. *Listening for the Heartbeat of God: A Celtic Spirituality*. New York: Paulist, 1997.

Park, Andrew Sung. *The Wounded Heart of God: The Asian Concept of Han and the Christian Doctrine of Sin*. Nashville: Abingdon, 1993.

Schwager, Raymund, and James G. Williams. *Banished from Eden: Original Sin and Evolutionary Theory in the Drama of Salvation*. Leominster, Herefordshire: Gracewing, 2006.

Smith, H. Shelton. *Changing Conceptions of Original Sin: A Study in American Theology since 1750*. New York: Scribner, 1955.

Stendahl, Krister. "The Apostle Paul and the Introspective Conscience of the West," *Harvard Theological Review* 56, no. 3 (1963): 199–215. *JSTOR*.

Suchocki, Marjorie. *The Fall to Violence: Original Sin in Relational Theology*. New York: Continuum, 1994.

Taylor, Charles. *Sources of the Self: The Making of the Modern Identity*. Cambridge, MA: Harvard University Press, 1989.

Toews, John E. *The Story of Original Sin*. Eugene, OR: Wipf & Stock, 2013.

Tutu, Desmond, Mpho A. Tutu, and Douglas Carlton Abrams. *Made for Goodness: And Why This Makes All the Difference*. New York: HarperOne, 2010.

Vorster, Nicolaas. *Created in the Image of God: Understanding God's Relationship with Humanity*. Eugene, OR: Pickwick, 2011.